The Smart Mission

The Smart Mission

NASA's Lessons for Managing Knowledge,
People, and Projects

Edward J. Hoffman, Matthew Kohut, and Laurence Prusak

The MIT Press

Cambridge, Massachusetts | London, England

The MIT Press would like to thank the anonymous peer reviewers who provided comments on drafts of this book. The generous work of academic experts is essential for establishing the authority and quality of our publications. We acknowledge with gratitude the contributions of these otherwise uncredited readers.

This book was set in Stone Serif and Stone Sans by Westchester Publishing Services. Printed and bound in the United States of America.

Library of Congress Cataloging-in-Publication Data

Names: Hoffman, Edward J. (Edward Jay), 1959- author. | Kohut, Matthew, author. | Prusak, Laurence, author.
Title: The smart mission : NASA's lessons for managing knowledge, people, and projects / Edward J. Hoffman, Matthew Kohut, and Laurence Prusak.
Description: Cambridge, Massachusetts : The MIT Press, [2022] | Includes bibliographical references and index.
Identifiers: LCCN 2021046198 | ISBN 9780262046886 (hardcover)
Subjects: LCSH: United States. National Aeronautics and Space Administration. | Organizational learning. | Knowledge management.
Classification: LCC HD58.82 .H627 2022 | DDC 658.4/038--dc23/eng/20211221
LC record available at https://lccn.loc.gov/2021046198

10 9 8 7 6 5 4 3 2 1

Contents

Introduction

The project is the basic unit of work for many of the largest and most complex organizations in the world. Whether the end result is a software application, antiviral vaccine, or spacecraft, a great deal of work today gets done at the project level. In a very real sense, we live in a project world. From blockbuster films to energy production, the project is the unit of organization for a significant share of global economic activity.

And yet projects are failing us because they are understood and defined in the wrong way. A project of any complexity is an effort to harness multidisciplinary expertise to solve challenges for the benefit of people. But the dominant paradigm of project management is one of control, processes, and tools. This disregards the human dimension—learning, collaboration, teaming, communication, and culture—that is intangible, hard to measure, and resistant to control.

Projects run on knowledge—a combination of learning and experience that enables people to perform tasks. A project can have all the resources in the world, but without the necessary knowledge it is doomed. There are plenty of other reasons that projects fail, but lack of know-how almost guarantees a bad outcome. This kind of knowledge is not a thing that can be found in a book or hoarded by an individual. It comes from experienced people working in a team setting.

Some organizations understand the interplay of knowledge, projects, and people better than others. This book will explore some of the intangible elements that inform projects and share insights about approaches and practices that successful organizations have adopted to address them so that others can consider new approaches to working and learning in a project environment.

Three leitmotifs recur throughout this book. The first is that projects are fundamentally about how teams work and learn together to get things done. Project teams are not like professional sports teams that play games with clearly defined rules. Project teams may rely on repeatable processes to design, build, test, and deliver products or services, but innovation, whether incremental or radical, depends on team learning. As Arie de Geus of Royal Dutch Shell Group writes, "The ability to learn faster than your competitors may be the only sustainable competitive advantage."[1]

Second, the local level is where the action happens. Innovations and breakthroughs that lead to project success rarely come from the top of large, centralized organizations. If anything, a burdensome bureaucracy will spur a project team to expend considerable time and energy finding ways to work around it. This is nothing new—the agile movement that began two decades ago has brought widespread recognition to the benefits of decentralized decision-making—but the implications for knowledge often go unnoticed. The governance of knowledge and projects in large organizations is typically most effective when it empowers people working at the local level to respond quickly to changing conditions.

Finally, projects don't operate in a vacuum. They exist within organizations that are responsible to stakeholders, whether they are corporations accountable to shareholders or government agencies accountable to political leaders and the public. A project's success or failure depends in large part on the health of this ecosystem.

Projects can vary so dramatically in complexity that it's useful to have models that help explain the dimensions of their knowledge needs. The traditional project management "iron triangle" of cost, schedule, and scope does little to articulate the differences between a project that delivers a sidewalk versus another that delivers a supercollider, let alone accounting for elements like knowledge, learning, communication, team dynamics, culture, or collaboration. We address these elements first by considering the environment at the organization, team, and individual levels.

There is a symbiotic relationship between an organization that pursues its mission through projects and the teams and individual members that execute them. The organization supports its teams and individuals by providing resources and infrastructure for knowledge and learning as well as a culture that shapes the work environment. This enables teams and individuals to learn and acquire the knowledge needed for their projects, which in turn increases the organization's capability for future projects.

We approach project complexity through the lens of knowledge and learning needs, identifying three project models—micro, macro, and global—that each operate on different knowledge chess boards.

A micro project seeks to solve a problem that is finite and primarily technical in nature. The challenge can be simple or difficult, but the solution comes as a result of having the right technical know-how to get the job done. The classical Greeks called this kind of knowledge *episteme*, or scientific knowledge based on repeatable rules. A micro project can be a straightforward software project such as delivering a feature for a website, or it can require a great deal of innovation (think of an ambitious R&D initiative), but in either case the project team has the authority and ability to focus on the technical challenge at hand. Politics is not front and center, though knowledge of people and processes plays an important part in getting things done.

The VITAL (Ventilator Intervention Technology Accessible Locally) project undertaken by the Jet Propulsion Laboratory (JPL) in the early days of the COVID-19 pandemic is an example of a micro project. An ad hoc team of National Aeronautics and Space Administration (NASA) engineers went from having no knowledge of medical devices or ventilators to delivering a working prototype of a ventilator that could be made from commercial off-the-shelf parts in 37 days. This crash course in acquiring technical know-how is a master class in rapid team learning. Although team members did manage stakeholder relationships with NASA headquarters and external partners such as Mt. Sinai Hospital and the Food and Drug Administration (FDA), the project's primary knowledge challenge was technical.

While the VITAL team had to develop and acquire its technical knowledge from scratch, the great asset it had from the start was local knowledge of how to run a successful project from concept to closeout. Its unique, time-sensitive mission coincided with pandemic-driven lockdowns, which meant the team primarily operated remotely and on its own. The project had the backing of JPL leadership, enabling the team to maintain a laser-like focus on its goal.

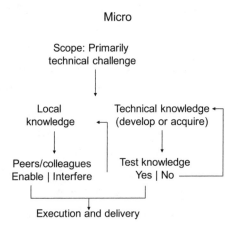

A macro project focuses on a problem that can only be solved by involving a significant part of an organization, ranging from a division or large business unit to the entire enterprise. The need for technical knowledge cannot be divorced from the organizational knowledge required to gain support for changes in resources, authority, or norms and behaviors. Mastery of organizational politics is necessary to secure buy-in from key decision makers and neutralize pockets of resistance. In addition to technical knowledge (*episteme*), a macro project requires street smarts (which the ancient Greeks called *metis*, a combination of cleverness and cunning) about the organization.

A macro project we will explore is one that Ed led in setting up an enterprise-wide knowledge capability for NASA across its many centers, mission directorates, and functional areas in response to direction from a congressionally backed advisory panel. From the outset, organizational friction was the greatest potential obstacle to success. Knowledge of the organization and its people and culture was far more important than subject matter expertise.

Ed and his team (which included Larry and Matt) already had the technical understanding necessary to address this challenge. The real work was in engaging stakeholders, understanding their capabilities and concerns, sharing insights with them about the nature of the problem at the agency-wide level, and ultimately earning their approval to move forward with a solution that was both flexible and binding.

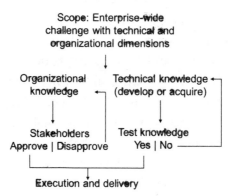

Macro

Scope: Enterprise-wide
challenge with technical and
organizational dimensions

Organizational knowledge → Technical knowledge (develop or acquire)

Stakeholders Approve | Disapprove   Test knowledge Yes | No

Execution and delivery

A global project addresses a vast societal challenge. This can be a public health problem like eradicating smallpox, or a knowledge quest such as unraveling scientific mysteries of the universe through a shared laboratory or observatory. Since these projects transcend national borders, they require the establishment of a new project ecosystem before an organization created for this purpose can begin to tackle the technical aspects of the problem. These projects are inherently political, and they call for practical wisdom about the way the world works (the Greeks called this worldliness *phronesis*—wisdom and prudence acting in the world) in combination with *metis* and *episteme*. They are akin to a three-dimensional chess game: critical knowledge can be identified at global, organizational, and local levels. Global knowledge—an understanding of a project's political dimension—is necessary to manage relationships among governments, corporations, universities, and other key stakeholders. Organizational knowledge is unique since the organization itself has to be created to execute the project. And local knowledge within the project is still just as essential as it is for a project with a narrower scope.

We dedicate a chapter to a case study of the international collaboration required to design, build, and operate the International Space Station (ISS), a one-of-a-kind project that remains a model of cooperation among partners that compete in other arenas. The working relationships that have emerged from the partnership are not the sum of the bilateral relationships among the various space agencies; they are the hard-won result of a shared sense of purpose.

Before there could be an ISS, the partners had to reach an agreement to work together toward a goal that no single country could achieve on its own. From a NASA perspective, this required the political knowledge necessary to build and maintain a new project environment that could serve this global mission while respecting the interests of each partner. NASA's ISS team then had to develop organizational knowledge about how to work effectively in this partnership in addition to addressing the myriad technical knowledge challenges of constructing a space station that would be continuously inhabited for years on end.

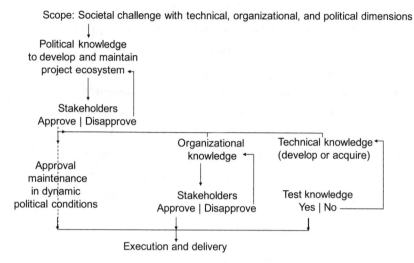

Global

Scope: Societal challenge with technical, organizational, and political dimensions

Political knowledge
to develop and maintain
project ecosystem

Stakeholders
Approve | Disapprove

Approval
maintenance
in dynamic
political conditions

Organizational
knowledge

Technical knowledge
(develop or acquire)

Stakeholders
Approve | Disapprove

Test knowledge
Yes | No

Execution and delivery

As these models suggest, technical knowledge is critical but insufficient unless the problem is essentially technical *and* the project team is empowered with the authority to solve it without interference. In our experience, complex projects rarely, if ever, have a purely technical focus. Yet few organizations acknowledge their need for organizational or political knowledge.

Global projects: Societal challenges with technical, organizational, and political dimensions that require international collaboration

Macro projects: Enterprise-wide challenges with technical and organizational dimensions

Micro projects: Primarily technical challenges

Knowledge and learning
infrastructure and governance

Knowledge and learning
opportunities and support

Organization ←——————→ Project Team ←——————→ Individual

COMMUNICATION

COMMUNICATION

CULTURE

Project-based organizations, whether they're companies, government agencies, or nongovernmental organizations, come in different shapes and sizes. Factors such as problem novelty, cost measurement, and point of customer involvement help to distinguish the kinds of projects an organization might sponsor. We offer three archetypes for organizations that accomplish their work through projects while acknowledging that most large organizations are hybrids that combine elements of more than one of these models.

A *complex project-based organization* is in the one-and-only business. These are organizations like NASA or CERN, the European Organization for Nuclear Research, that solve fundamentally novel problems. Cost and schedule are measured in terms of the project life cycle rather than a unit of production (e.g., the time and dollars required to manufacture a single automobile in a mass-production operation). The customer, which in the case of NASA or CERN is often a team of scientists seeking to run highly sophisticated experiments and collect data, is typically involved throughout the life cycle because of the complexity of the problem. Success is impossible without significant technology development and innovation.

A *mass-production organization* is a manufacturer working at scale, whether it makes cars or candy bars. Problems in production are measured, scored for criticality, and tracked until resolved. These organizations use lean or agile methodologies to improve quality and efficiency and have a separate research and development (R&D) function focused on breakthrough innovations. Customer feedback informs the design and production process, but the point of sale is where most customers enter the picture.

An *entrepreneurial organization* in this framework is something like a pure software-as-a-service (SaaS) organization, for example. The minimum viable product provides the initial basis for continuous testing and improvement, which is informed by ongoing customer feedback. Since there are no per-unit physical capital costs as there are with cars or candy bars, the unit cost goes down with every subsequent sale.

These distinctions are useful when thinking about how organizations work with knowledge. Since knowledge is inherently social, the structure of an organization plays a huge role in its approach to knowledge development, retention, and transfer.

Three Models for Project-Based Organizations

	Complex Project-Based Organization	Mass-Production Organization	Entrepreneurial Organization
Product	One-and-only	Scalable manufacture	Permanent beta
Problems	Novel	Measurable	Hackable
Technology	New/invented	R&D > innovate Lean or agile > improve	Minimum viable product
Cost	Life cycle	Unit	Zero marginal
Schedule	Project completion	Productivity rate	Iterative
Customer	Involved at inception	Involved at point of sale	Involved in testing
Knowledge Need	Innovation + limited production	Innovation + continuous improvement	Bootstrap + innovation

Why this book now? Most books about project management are written for academics rather than practitioners—they are strong on theory and advice but short on real-life application. None that we know of focus on the relationship between projects and knowledge. The missing ingredient is people. Knowledge is a social phenomenon. Team dynamics and organizational considerations including governance, incentives, and culture can either promote or inhibit the learning and collaboration necessary for project success. There isn't a neat algorithm for optimal performance in project-based organizations; the intangibles make all the difference. Even so, we have sought to identify enabling practices that can help organizations and teams reckon with those intangibles.

This book is about missions—assignments or tasks with a defined purpose or objective—specifically missions undertaken by project teams, organizations, or societies. The three coauthors collectively spent over 60 years supporting one of the world's preeminent mission-driven organizations—NASA. While our assignments ranged from tackling challenges of strategic governance to the creation of knowledge systems to talent development for project and program-based teams, the consistent purpose was to help create successful project teams in advance of mission need.

The term *successful* is tricky. It speaks to value and implies factors such as performance, cost, timeliness, scientific achievement, and public recognition. Perceptions of mission success can change over time. The Hubble Space Telescope began as a spectacular, high-visibility failure, and through a process of adaptive response to changing conditions became a cherished symbol of excellence.

We believe that all missions can be smart. A smart mission recognizes that few things go as planned, and that both learning and unlearning are essential. It understands that knowledge creation happens at the team level, and therefore works to design and sustain a strong, inclusive team that collaborates effectively. It is conscious of the culture it develops and maintains. Above all, it values people, and offers them the opportunity to be part of something that has meaning and purpose.

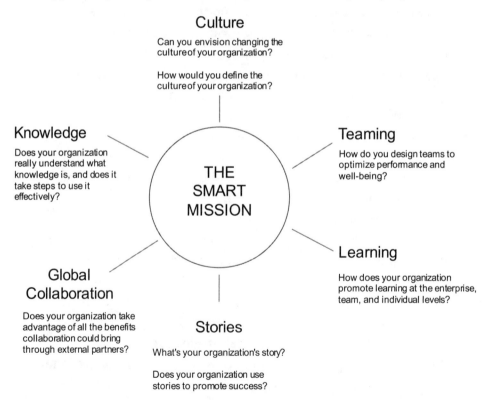

The authors have decades of experience understanding knowledge and projects. Ed trained as a social psychologist and then spent 33 years with NASA, founding its project academy and retiring as its first chief knowledge officer. During his last decade at NASA, he brought in Larry and Matthew to help the agency address some of its challenges related to knowledge and project management. Larry is one of the world's leading authorities on the subject of knowledge in organizations, having written nine books and more than 50 articles and consulted with more than 300 organizations around the globe on the topic. Matthew has run a consultancy focused on learning and development for over a decade and has written widely about leadership, communication, and influence.

Our shared experience with NASA gives us a unique perspective, but this book is not solely about NASA. Ed and Larry teach in Columbia University's Information and Knowledge Strategy program, and all three authors currently serve as senior advisers to the Project Management Institute. We've drawn from our networks to interview experts from a wide variety of organizations and sectors who have challenged and broadened our thinking, and we shared individual anecdotes about work with a variety of organizations.

During Ed's tenure at NASA, the entities he led that were tasked with building project management capability evolved. The initial Program/Project Management Initiative, founded in the wake of the space shuttle *Challenger* accident, focused primarily on training and developing individual competence. The subsequent NASA Academy of Program/Project Leadership, which later became today's NASA Academy of Program/Project & Engineering Leadership, expanded the scope of activity to address team learning and knowledge effectiveness at the individual, team, and organizational levels. For the sake of simplicity, we will refer to all of these as "the NASA project academy" throughout the book.

There is no all-encompassing definition of a project academy. Around the same time that Ed was establishing one at NASA in the mid-1990s, other organizations including Shell, Rolls Royce,

Siemens, and Fujitsu were setting up their own academies.[2] Many shared common high-level goals such as promoting consistency in project management capability across their organizations, but each organization's approach and offerings varied widely. NASA's project academy evolved over roughly a decade from a project management training program for individuals to a diversified learning organization that provided a range of services to support project teams and promote knowledge sharing across the organization. We will go into detail about the project academy's offerings in several chapters.

We begin in the first chapter by focusing on knowledge. What types and categories of knowledge prove most critical to project success? We'll explore the social nature of knowledge and the implications for teams and organizations. A decade ago, NASA underwent a significant enterprise-level transformation of its approach to knowledge. This came in response to stakeholder pressure on NASA to improve its ability to share knowledge openly across the agency. The hidden challenge that many organizations face is addressing the social factors that inhibit this flow of knowledge.

Learning is the other side of the coin from knowledge: it is an activity whereby knowledge is specifically taught and transferred to others. Most organizations emphasize learning at an individual level, which is insufficient in a context that demands team learning and organizational infrastructure and support. Chapter 2 looks at the ways NASA developed and expanded opportunities for learning at the individual, team, and organizational levels.

Chapter 3 will examine how NASA used stories to present and develop new ideas and transfer existing ideas to its workforce of civil servants and contractors. Venues for stories included *ASK Magazine*, a practitioner-based publication devoted to knowledge and innovation, and live forums dedicated to sharing new ideas from within and outside of NASA. We will go into detail as to how, after a great deal of skepticism, stories became an accepted and very potent tool for sharing knowledge at NASA. Other organizations have had success using stories in a similar fashion.

Efforts to improve knowledge sharing and learning cannot be successful unless the organization values and recognizes the importance of these activities. This understanding comes from the culture of the organization. Chapter 4 explores what it takes to develop a knowledge-based culture. We will discuss some of the dynamics that helped contribute to this at NASA as well as exploring other organizations that have addressed this issue.

Since project work is done in teams, the composition, dynamics, and knowledge capabilities of teams are critical to success. Project performance takes place at the team level. Chapter 5 addresses these issues and examines how NASA revamped its approach to enhancing team performance to meet the extraordinary demands of its projects.

Projects are increasingly global, and the International Space Station is one of the most ambitious and successful projects in history. Chapter 6 begins with the challenge of developing a partnership in order to facilitate this project. NASA's work with other countries, especially Russia, was difficult due to international politics as well as cultural and organizational differences. The space station serves as a case study of overcoming political, cultural, and organizational differences in the name of advancing knowledge to benefit humanity.

We conclude by synthesizing lessons about the linkages between knowledge and projects, and by looking to the future of learning as technologies such as artificial intelligence begin to reshape the future of work. As we write this during the COVID-19 global pandemic, the need for international collaboration to tackle the world's most pressing challenges has never been more urgent. The social dimension of knowledge and the need for people to collaborate will remain constant even as projects become increasingly complex and pose technical challenges that we can't anticipate today.

1
Knowledge

Knowledge is the source of wealth. Applied to tasks we already
know, it becomes productivity. Applied to tasks that are new, it
becomes innovation.
　　　　　—Peter F. Drucker, *Peter F. Drucker on Practical Leadership*

Toward the end of 2011, Mike Ryschkewitsch, NASA's chief engineer,
called Ed into his office for a meeting. As Ed entered, he noticed the
agency's senior engineering leaders sitting around the table. He saw
a big binder stuffed with recommendations from a congressionally
mandated oversight panel focused on safety. One of the panel's recommendations concerned the need for an enterprise-wide approach
to knowledge management. The discussion that followed focused on
how NASA should respond to this recommendation. As the meeting
wrapped up, Ed said, "I am happy to consult and help out in any way
possible, as long as I am not appointed the NASA chief knowledge
officer." The oversight panel had explicitly called for the establishment of this new position.

　　Ed was not kidding. He loved his role as the founding director of
NASA's project academy.[1] He also knew the knowledge community

across NASA's ten centers was both talented and conflict-ridden. The last thing he wanted was to be the antagonist in a turf war. His other consideration was whether NASA's leadership would support a formal, integrated knowledge program. After more than 25 years at NASA, he was politically savvy enough to realize that "critical" programs often started in response to short-term priorities, only to be killed a year or two later. The odds were always against a new initiative.

About two weeks later, Mike poked his head into Ed's office and asked if they could talk alone. Ed waited for the hammer to drop.

"We need you to be the NASA CKO," the chief engineer said.

Ed took a deep breath and communicated his support to do whatever NASA needed. He told Mike that he wanted to meet with Chris Scolese, the associate administrator, to understand how his leadership viewed the importance of the position.

That afternoon, he received a call from a colleague at one of NASA's centers:

"We hear a rumor that HQ is considering establishing a CKO."

"What do you think of the idea?" Ed asked.

"It's a stupid idea. Headquarters doesn't know a thing about managing knowledge. It will destroy the progress we have made so far!"

"Well, we will just have to see what will happen."

"The other rumor is that you will be the new CKO."

"What do you think of that?"

"That would be a shame."

"Why?"

"We really like you. It would be a shame to have to kill you at this point in your career."

The next day he sat down across from Chris Scolese, a former boss who was now NASA's top civil servant. Ed shared his concerns openly and explained that his focus would be on the people side of the equation, saying, "There are many in the knowledge management community who see knowledge management from a technology, process, and tools perspective. That is important, but it will not be my starting point."

"We're good with that. We need this to work. You are respected by the engineering and project community. If your name is attached to this, it will signal NASA is serious about this effort."

That was what Ed needed to hear. NASA's senior leaders were firmly behind this. They understood the importance of the social capital Ed had built over 25 years. Ed had spent much of his career at NASA establishing networks focused on learning and knowledge, and these efforts now gave him the necessary credibility and trust to establish the role of chief knowledge officer in a way that would lead his colleagues in the knowledge community to cooperate rather than resist. Even if they had suspicions about the idea, the good will from those longstanding relationships would be a big advantage. His managers also saw that the approach he had taken to building the project academy had laid the groundwork for an enterprise-wide knowledge initiative.

Ed had a broad understanding of knowledge after more than a decade of convening NASA practitioners from various disciplines to share their experience and lessons with each other. He grasped the social and contextual nature of knowledge. It was clear to him from the outset that the challenge NASA faced was more about *who* than *what*.

What Do We Mean by Knowledge?

One of the many perplexing things about knowledge is the sheer number of definitions for the word. We have asked people in seminars and workshops to define the word, and their answers always vary widely. Some think it is another name for useful information, and others believe it means having volumes of data at one's command.

The Greeks in their classical writings used at least eight different words for what we call knowledge, and even today many languages use at least two. For example, in French, *savoir* means science and other more scholarly endeavors, while *connaissance* is usually used for knowledge as acquaintance, familiarity, or information. The limitation of using one word in English leads to confusion when trying to set up "knowledge systems" or "capture" knowledge.

Knowledge is not information, although information can be seen as a piece of knowledge when it is added to an individual's store of know-what. Knowledge isn't data or wisdom either. A few years ago, Larry was asked by a reporter for a quick definition that would help people understand the differences between these terms. He came up with this: Let's say you plan to make a fine dinner for someone you care for. The letters in a printed recipe are data, the recipe is information, knowledge is the ability to cook, and wisdom is marrying a good cook.

For our purposes in this book, we are talking here about *working knowledge*—the type of knowledge that underlies practices and activities in everyday life and allows one to perform both simple and complex tasks. It is earned through a combination of experiences informed by reflective learning and is often difficult to fully articulate. It often comes from participating in actions with others in performing tasks, projects, and other collaborative acts. Working knowledge is a mix of explicit and tacit knowledge, or know-what and know-how, with a stronger dose of the latter. Perhaps it is easier to understand it as a craft, or a practice, as in the practice of medicine, law, or engineering. In any case, we tend to know it when we encounter it.

It takes time and experience to become truly knowledgeable. A student fresh out of college with a bachelor's degree in chemistry is not a chemist. She has absorbed a great deal of information about chemistry and likely spent some time in a laboratory, but would other chemists call her a chemist? Very unlikely. She would need to actually *do* chemistry—gain lived experience through working and rubbing elbows with other chemists. She must practice chemistry to become a practitioner. Only then could she claim working knowledge of the subject.

Knowledge is a slippery word because it describes something that is basically intangible, though the outcomes of it are often plain to see, and those outcomes enable us to determine its value and best uses. Whether we are discussing a car, medicine, legal advice, or the space shuttle, we can value its performance and outcome without trying to meticulously identify the knowledge that went into creating it. But it is useful and important to understand the *sources* of an organization's knowledge to get a better grip on what it does and doesn't know, and how to use that knowledge in a more effective way.

Knowledge is profoundly social. Individual knowledge is important, but it pales in comparison to the knowledge of a group. This can be true of a team, network, community of practice, or any other aggregate unit where there is a generalized common goal, vocabulary, understanding, and purpose. Members of groups such as these inspire and aid one another, and new solutions and ideas often emerge from group activities ranging from formal and informal meetings to simply working together.

Ideas about the nature of knowledge are deeply influenced by the culture of the person using it. "We find knowledge inseparable from the knower," says Naoki Ogiwara, managing director of a Tokyo-based global consulting firm that specializes in knowledge.[2] He notes that in East Asian cultures, knowledge is viewed "not as a thing to be measured, but an attribute or force within us." In Western cultures and those regions most influenced by the West, knowledge is often thought of as something that can be expressed in a rule or an algorithm, or embedded in a form external to the knower. These two very different understandings of how knowledge is manifested have created some difficulties in communications about how to successfully manage knowledge.

In recent years, however, practitioners have managed to combine both ideas when developing knowledge programs. This is largely because many managers and executives in larger organizations in Asia have either studied knowledge and learning in Western business schools (or their satellite branches in Asia) or had access to translations of Western texts on these topics. This exposure, in combination with the infusion of Western consulting firm models, has led to the emergence of hybrid models that incorporate both views of this subject.[3]

Knowledge Priorities for Organizations

In 2019, after an intensive period of exploration and research, the government of Abu Dhabi established the Early Childhood Authority (ECA), which is dedicated to supporting child development from conception to age eight for all children throughout the emirate. As the ECA undertook this long-range multidisciplinary challenge, its leaders understood the importance of building an ecosystem that would support four primary areas of focus: health and nutrition, child protection, family support, and early care and education. They recognized the need for both the latest global expertise about early childhood development as well as local knowledge about parents, children, and families in Abu Dhabi.

The knowledge the ECA needs to execute its mission cannot be found in a report by the World Bank or United Nations. It has to be developed by a team that understands how to function as a government institution in its unique political culture, and how to navigate the sociocultural context of Abu Dhabi when advocating for changes in early childhood development. As a new organization, it is still building its stock of working knowledge. "There's a lot of work to be done," says H. E. Sana Mohamad Suhail, leader of the ECA's founding team.[4] With a mission that will take years to show results in some areas, much of the working knowledge it is acquiring now will be replaced by 2035, the time horizon set out in its founding strategy. New knowledge almost always grows from past knowledge, as it often appropriates and modifies the ideas of the past that are still useful.

Working knowledge can be embodied in people and embedded in processes and routines. When a new idea enters an organization it is evaluated, and if deemed valuable, it takes root as a part of the way work is organized and performed until a better idea supersedes it. It becomes part of the set of routines and processes that allows an organization to operate.

An example common to many firms over the past few decades is the adoption of lean or agile processes. The knowledge of how these processes work typically comes from outside the organization, undergoes an evaluation and adaptation process, and then becomes part of the way work gets done. The adaptation process is a strategy of experimentation. Some experiments succeed and become the basis for new practices, while others fail and serve as lessons to inform future experiments.

When organizations decide to actively engage with knowledge, they generally focus on three activities: *knowledge development, knowledge retention,* and *knowledge transfer and diffusion.* All of these activities are critical to any organization, but their value and the time spent on any of them largely depend on the organization's products or services. Most organizations in our experience choose one or maybe two of these activities to focus on.

Knowledge development focuses on how knowledge comes into an organization, is evaluated, and becomes part of an organization's stock of working knowledge. This can be done by forming an alliance with a firm that has needed knowledge, buying that firm outright, hiring consultants or other advisors, or creating a team or task force to identify new sources of knowledge.

For example, when IBM realized that organizational learning was going to be an important part of most of its client organizations' operations, they found that they had no particular expertise in developing tools for this activity. The market for such tools was moving quickly, and a delay in entering that marketplace would be a commercial error. IBM decided to buy Lotus Development Co., which had resources including Lotus Notes, a pioneering collaboration tool, and the Lotus Institute, which studied organizational learning. This group became successfully integrated into IBM's strategy and operations, and its practical working knowledge was now available to the entire firm.

Sometimes new knowledge emerges through serendipitous discovery that brings forth something local and unheralded within an organization. This happened at NASA when trying to mitigate a risk within the space shuttle program before shuttle launch STS-119 in March 2010. The technical tool that ultimately helped leaders understand the risk was developed by a quiet engineer whose efforts may have gone unnoticed without proactive leadership that reached out to employees who might not be inclined to volunteer their thoughts in meetings. Steve Altemus, director of engineering at Johnson Space Center at the time, said, "It's important to recognize that we're not always the smartest one in the room, that perhaps there's somebody over there in the corner of the room, and that we have to pull out of them what their thoughts are, because they've got the answer."[5]

Knowledge retention is usually associated with training and internal learning processes in order to embody knowledge in chosen employees. The effectiveness of these processes is mixed. As we explain in chapter 2, a great deal of knowledge retention happens directly and informally among employees as circumstances allow. But a growing trend in knowledge retention is the development of academies and corporate universities. These entities have proven to be very successful for several reasons, such as their tendency to hire highly qualified academics as instructors. For example, Apple University hired Joel Podolny, a former dean of the Yale School of Management who previously taught at Harvard and Stanford, and it has lured several similarly credentialed academics to its faculty since then. Microsoft has made comparable efforts. These academies have commonalities that distinguish them from traditional training. They use far more interactive teaching methods, and their instructors are more experienced than those who typically lead corporate training courses. Attendance is often voluntary, and at organizations like NASA, Apple, and others it can be a badge of honor to be chosen to attend certain courses that pass on highly valued institutional knowledge.

Knowledge transfer or diffusion describes how knowledge gets intentionally shared among people or groups. This can happen at any level and degree of cardinality within an organization, whether it's one-to-one, one-to-many, or team-to-team. Many managers, organization theorists, and economists assume that if part of an organization (e.g., a division or team) has some knowledge, it is known by the whole organization. Needless to say, this isn't true. For varied reasons, knowledge is sticky—it tends to remain where it has been developed.[6]

Many knowledge-sharing efforts overlook the impediments to transferring knowledge, such as the reliability of the knowledge being transferred, logistical factors, the sheer difficulties of communicating and appropriating what is often complex and tacit, and the transaction costs that transferring knowledge can entail. We have learned that a great deal of knowledge transfer happens informally through casual or spontaneous conversations that spark new connections. A critical lesson shared in an email (or worse, a lessons-learned database) is less likely to find its audience than if it is shared in a discussion that allows listeners to prod, question, and evaluate the knowledge before deciding to act on it.

This should not be misinterpreted as a dismissal of the importance of documentation. Ray Ryan, a senior software engineer at Square, emphasizes the importance of capturing ideas in writing to facilitate knowledge transfer through dialogue. "The main thing is to write things down, teach others to write things down, and be willing to read what others have written down," he says. "The conversations we have are about the documents."[7] The critical distinction is that knowledge captured in writing is most likely to prove its value when it spurs conversation.

One way to encourage knowledge transfer is to build social infrastructures that allow employees to share what they know. Organizations that provide *spaces* to learn demonstrate a different level of understanding about the inherently social nature of knowledge. This concept is well known in Japan, and there is a Japanese word, *ba*, that is used to describe a space where common meaning is created.[8] The Swiss pharma giant Novartis rebuilt many of its antiquated buildings in Basel with a desire to increase serendipitous encounters in very open spaces throughout the buildings. This aim was aided by architects and consultants who specialized in spaces that encourage knowledge exchanges.[9] Apple also worked to design its latest headquarters in Cupertino with spaces for off-the-cuff conversations and chance meetings where people might bump into one another.[10] This drew on Steve Jobs's earlier inspiration when designing Pixar headquarters to locate the restrooms in an atrium in the center of the building for the same reason.[11] Today, many high-tech workplaces have coffee bars and pods for lounge chairs, but these spaces only matter if people feel free to use them as designed.

Where spaces are concerned, design matters. The adoption of open floor plan offices over the last decade may have grown out of the intention of fostering more collaboration and conversation among employees, but studies have found that in many open workplaces this has backfired. High ambient noise levels make concentration difficult, leading to greater stress levels and, paradoxically, increased reliance on email and instant messaging.[12]

Beyond physical spaces, events can offer a different kind of space for knowledge transfer. NASA has used this approach extensively, combining internal and external speakers to stir the pot of knowledge circulation while leaving ample time for talking, informal meetings, and conversation. Convening a workshop to reflect on and capture lessons learned from a project is a common example. As NASA approached the end of the space shuttle program, the project academy convened a series of knowledge-sharing sessions that addressed a wide range of themes spanning the multidecade lifecycle of the program. Virtual events can provide a similar space for dialogue, though informal interactions get lost in this setting.

Another way to transfer and diffuse knowledge is to relocate employees who have specific knowledge to places where this knowledge is needed. While this sounds simple, it has proven to be problematic since global firms often meet resistance when shuffling workers across the globe. Another impediment to this is that knowledge is not only sticky, as noted previously, but it is often context dependent: an idea may work well in one occupational or geographical context but not in another.

Several large energy firms have moved their knowledge by moving people. BP, which was one of the first large global firms to consciously implement knowledge programs, used this method to its advantage when it transferred workers with deepwater drilling expertise from the South China Sea to the Gulf of Mexico. Although BP had ample documentation and communication tools to spread this knowledge already and it faced the challenge of managing strong cultural differences among workers, the value of live demonstrations and collaboration on highly innovative techniques enabled the most immediate knowledge transfer possible.

Identifying Critical Knowledge

Though it would seem self-evident that "capturing" or even roughly identifying all the knowledge in any organization of size would be absurd, if not impossible, it has been attempted by several organizations. Much of this absurdity stems from three fallacies. The most common is the myth that enterprise-wide software promoted by vendors and consultants can either catalog the knowledge of the organization or serve as a portal for individual employees to share their knowledge. The latter, while having some value, is based on the false premise that individual knowledge is the most important unit of analysis in an organization.

The second fallacy is the belief (again promoted by technology vendors and consultants) that organizational knowledge is an objective, tangible "thing" that can be identified, manipulated, and harnessed in encyclopedic form. One famous example is Chrysler, which in the late 1980s developed "Engineering Books of Knowledge" for its automobile platform teams at considerable expense. Absent the context needed to understand the lessons in the system, much of their meaning was lost.[13] The main problems here, as with many other similar failed efforts, were that the unit of analysis was far too granular, and there was too much focus on tacit knowledge that couldn't be codified. Trying to document individual knowledge in a large industrial enterprise is futile.

NASA instead focused on the capabilities of each of its ten centers and mission directorates. For instance, Stennis Space Center in Mississippi has extensive expertise in rocket engine testing, while Johnson Space Center in Houston is the primary knowledge hub for human space flight. As part of Ed's agency-wide efforts, the knowledge professionals from these centers and mission directorates met periodically to build relationships and improve understanding of agency-wide capabilities.

The third misguided notion is that knowledge can be captured. This idea, which still has some currency, conflates knowledge with information. In the 1990s, there was a popular belief that if an organization could deliver the right information to the right person at the right time, the firm would prosper forever. This is a category error based on a misunderstanding of the nature of knowledge. Library-like information management systems can be incredibly useful, but they don't have much to do with knowledge.

Utopian fantasies about knowledge are widespread, and most are based on the notion that if an organization knows what it knows, it can gain an unbeatable competitive advantage. This idea has superseded the older idea that if an organization could get the right information to the right person at the right time, it would solve the riddle. None of this is accurate. To know what an organization actually knows would take a far more complex and sophisticated system of identifying *who* knows what, and where they are. Systems like this have been built by the likes of McKinsey and Goldman Sachs, and many consulting and legal firms, and they have been successful in making their internal market for knowledge far more effective and efficient. Even so, most organizations continue to make the mistake of focusing on "what" rather than "who."

Despite all these notes of caution, there are compelling reasons for any organization to try to identify, locate, and evaluate the value, currency, and accessibility of its critical knowledge. The key to making this worthwhile is understanding knowledge needs as dynamic rather than static. If dynamic capabilities represent an organization's ability "to integrate, build, and reconfigure internal and external competences to address rapidly changing environments," as researchers have suggested, it's hard to imagine any organization having those capabilities without grasping the underlying knowledge structures that support them.[14]

Not all knowledge is critical for effective performance capability. Much depends on an organization's products or services, the complexity involved with product or service delivery, and the competitiveness of the market. NASA used the term "mission-critical knowledge" to describe this distinction. The process of identifying what's truly critical doesn't need to be difficult. The best way we know to explore this is through a series of questions, such as "What do we know that enables us to do well?" and "What do we need to know that we don't know right now?" See the "Putting Knowledge to Work" section at the end of this chapter for a list of questions that can serve as a starting point.

The level of granularity is also important to consider. What is the unit of analysis when evaluating critical knowledge? It is almost never an individual, since knowledge is a social activity. NASA identified agency-level leadership teams that had a direct connection to organizational strategy as its principal unit, whereas other firms have used departments, networks, communities, task forces, and other aggregate measures. The unit of analysis is often driven by organizational incentives. In organizations that reward employees for publishing reports, for instance, the report becomes the unit of analysis rather than the team that produces the report. Gaining clarity about this can lead to productive conversations about the difference between knowledge outputs and outcomes.

Knowledge Economics

While there is consensus today among economists that knowledge is critically important to any organization, there is still not as much research and analysis on this subject as would be expected for such a valuable entity. MIT's Robert Gibbons, an authority on organizational economics, says, "There are glaring gaps between the topics organizational economics has addressed and the productivity of real organizations. Perhaps the biggest gap concerns knowledge."[15] Much of this can be attributed to three factors.

First, as mentioned earlier, knowledge is an intangible asset, among other key intangibles such as culture, morale, trust, and what John Maynard Keynes deemed the *animal spirits*—a contagious sense of positive optimism that lives outside the laws of mathematical probability.[16] The intangible nature of knowledge makes it very hard to measure, and measurement lies at the heart of economics. The inherently social nature of knowledge makes it almost impossible to quantify, though interesting work has begun in the area of social network analysis. But the number of PhDs in a firm tells you nothing about its critical knowledge.

Second, there is no commonly agreed-on unit of analysis. Economists can measure stocks and flows of information at the level of a nation or a network, but without a common unit for knowledge, they have not ventured very far into this field. This has led to substitutes that are not always very accurate. There are ways to account for intellectual property, such as numbers of patents or publications, and there are substitutes such as money spent on training or information technologies, but none do a particularly good job of demonstrating the economic value of knowledge. Think of the knowledge possessed by Xerox PARC in the late 1970s that Steve Jobs was able to unlock at Apple just a few years later. How could an economist have valued that accurately at the time?

Third, for many industries, knowledge is more of an intermediate good than the final product of an organization. Think of a car manufacturer, for instance. The firm depends on a stream of new and existing knowledge, but the cars are the ultimate output that matters. For consulting firms, universities, think tanks, and others, though, knowledge *is* the product, so the unit of analysis is often the development of new knowledge that can be evaluated, sold, or used as a public good. NASA is an interesting exception to this because research and development is central to its mission as a public organization: the knowledge produced is as important as the actual rockets, spacecraft, and instruments.

While it is hard for economists to identify the value of knowledge, there are many studies on the costs associated with it—especially the costs of knowledge transfer. Knowledge doesn't flow like water or move as quickly and cheaply as information and data. Since knowledge is social, the transaction cost is primarily a function of the total time it takes to identify, locate, evaluate, and adapt knowledge. The time it takes to search for a source of knowledge represents a relatively small part of the total cost. Larry and his colleague Al Jacobson found that 80 percent of the time spent acquiring new knowledge is consumed by the process of eliciting it from people and then adapting it for a specific context.[17] The real drivers of the cost are social. In global organizations, time and space can constrain the ability to have live conversations, as can barriers related to organizational culture and incentives. A highly competitive culture can discourage sharing if employees guard knowledge in order to maintain an advantage over others, or if time spent sharing will take away from their own work.

Knowledge Governance

After becoming NASA's first chief knowledge officer, Ed faced the challenge of establishing an agency-wide approach to knowledge that would increase NASA's overall knowledge capability, satisfy the agency's external stakeholders who had called for action, and earn the cooperation of knowledge leads at different centers and organizations within NASA. The existing knowledge programs across NASA varied widely, ranging from bare-bones initiatives to complex technology-based systems. Some of its centers, mission directorates, and functional offices shared freely, while others were more like gated communities. Ed already knew that any effort to centralize these programs would be dead on arrival. At the same time, agency-wide coordination and sharing had to become the new norm in order to make progress.

As he planned to convene the first in-person meeting of the NASA knowledge communities—employees who already had some responsibility for knowledge in specific parts of the organization—Ed aimed to secure agreement on a set of guiding principles that were broad enough to feel inclusive and specific enough to result in positive change. By the end of that meeting, the community had reached consensus on five points that would ultimately serve as the kernel for an agency-wide governance model for knowledge:

We recognize that knowledge is embedded in the flow of all the work we do in order to get real results.

We foster community-wide knowledge acquisition, access, sharing, and reuse.

We respect local customs while enhancing organizational norms.

We strive to operationalize and brand knowledge so that it resonates with all stakeholders—what it is, what it isn't, and how to use it effectively.

We collaborate across organizational boundaries, remove stovepipes, and continuously measure our effectiveness (people, process, systems).

The governance model that NASA's knowledge community adopted was a *federated system*. The chief virtue of a federated system is that it provides a means for addressing organizational politics and competing interests.[18] At NASA, this model endorsed the value of the local knowledge held by the centers while granting the opportunity to let each center take advantage of what the others were doing. It also ensured representation of each center to NASA's senior management. And it avoided the dangers Ed foresaw with a centralized, or *monarchical* approach, while achieving greater unity than a *feudal* system in which local leaders controlled access and no common language existed across the organization.

It is useful to stress here that the governance structure for managing organizational knowledge needs to fit the culture and the strategy of the organization as well as the national or regional culture in which it is located. Some organizations such as intelligence agencies have a strong need for monarchy, and organizations that have a number of disparate major products or decentralized sites may be best suited for feudalism.

Having reached agreement on a federated governance structure, the community committed to mapping an inventory of knowledge assets across the agency, and to developing a knowledge policy that reflected the guiding principles. These activities served as building blocks for establishing NASA's agency-wide approach to knowledge. They were based on a reasonable understanding of the capabilities of each center or mission directorate. As CKO, Ed's primary roles were facilitating integration of these knowledge communities and advocating on their behalf to NASA's senior leadership and external stakeholders. At the second meeting of the knowledge community, Billy McMillan, a young professional from Kennedy Space Center who had been invited to participate, offered an observation that reflected a sophisticated understanding of knowledge: "[The solution is] not a system. You don't need software. It's our way of interacting with each other that needs to change."[19]

10 Principles for Working with Knowledge

1. Knowledge is a profoundly social and human activity. It may be represented in a process, rule, or system, but it is basically a human activity. It includes judgment, discernment, and a rich understanding that isn't yet accessible to machines, except as instructed by humans.

2. Knowledge is its own thing. It is not anything else. Knowledge isn't information or data or wisdom. It's a way of understanding a bounded subject that allows practitioners to act on that understanding.

3. Knowledge is temporal. It changes as new knowledge is developed and displaces old knowledge. This has always been true since the dawn of human achievements. Even with the most

established knowledge, such as Newton's laws, questions have been raised about their "truth" value, and several of them have been modified in the last century.

4.   Knowledge can be observed and understood but not captured. It is always largely tacit, and this type of tacit know-how can't be readily documented or captured by observation.

5.   Knowledge is expensive. It takes time, energy, and focus to become knowledgeable in a subject. There are no shortcuts to knowledge. One may have flash intuitions, but even those are dependent on prior knowledge for their efficacy.

6.   People, ideas, and things are all that we have. (This is a simple way of summarizing a powerful concept identified by economist Paul Romer.) A century ago, the world ran primarily on things— tangible objects ranging from pairs of shoes to barrels of oil. Things are still important, but our global economy is increasingly based on ideas that can be captured in algorithms, apps, drug developments, and financial tools, to name just a few examples.

7.   There is no individual knowledge—only individual memories. No one has useful knowledge that isn't known by others. Knowledge is a social construct that is tested by experience.

8.   Knowledge can be best understood and characterized as "know-what and know-how." Most people know that Paris is the capital of France—that is know-what. But an understanding of French culture or even the best ways to get around the city requires know-how.

9.   Experience doesn't automatically turn into knowledge. It needs to be framed and socialized and used in action.

10. Knowledge is an interdisciplinary subject. It can be approached and analyzed from almost all the social sciences and many of the humanities. The challenge is that the vocabularies and research agendas of the various disciplines within the social sciences and

humanities make it difficult to converge on general theoretical statements about knowledge.

Putting Knowledge to Work

What can practitioners do to gain an understanding of their organization's knowledge or improve its knowledge practices? Here are some suggestions.

Pick a unit of analysis that corresponds to places or structures that can be identified as knowledge hubs or hot spots that have an impact on business outcomes or strategy. There is usually some focused aggregate, such as a team, network, community, branch, division, or department. It is helpful to limit the unit to no more than 150 people, since that is the number of people any individual can know well socially. (This is known as Dunbar's Number, named for anthropologist Robin Dunbar.)

Identify critical knowledge, keeping in mind that knowledge is social and intangible rather than a "thing" that can be captured. These questions can serve as a starting point for discussion:

Strengths: What gives us a competitive advantage?

What do we know that enables us to do well?

What do we know that sets us apart from others?

Gaps: What opportunities and vulnerabilities can we see?

What do we need to know that we don't know right now?

What do we need to learn to do differently?

What do we know now that we could lose in the future?

Development: How do we develop new knowledge?

Innovation: Where do new ideas come from?

How well does the organization innovate?

How well does the team innovate?

Learning

   How well does the organization support learning?

   How well does the team support learning?

Problem-solving

   How well does the organization solve unexpected problems?

   How well does the project team solve unexpected problems?

Retention: How do we embed what we know in order to keep it?

Transfer: How do we share what we know across the organization?

   What incentives promote sharing and learning?

   What knowledge transaction costs can we identify?

      What incentives discourage sharing and learning?

      Do employees have time to share what they know?

      Do employees have spaces to share what they know?

Identify a governance model for knowledge that reflects the structure of your organization. Federated models are increasingly the norm in large, decentralized organizations. Centralized models (e.g., "monarchies") can work in settings where it's impossible to reach the consensus needed in a federated model as long as the culture and incentives foster open sharing. Above all, the governance model should align with and reflect the organization's culture.

Remember that ideas don't speak for themselves. Organizations are not meritocracies when it comes to adopting ideas. The decision makers in a hierarchy make the decisions, and their motives are almost always more complex than the pure potential value of the idea. Even before an idea reaches the C-suite, it needs to be sold. (Yes, sold.) This happens through conversation and influence. People who package ideas successfully know that the messenger is as important as the message. Identifying and cultivating champions with good reputations and strong networks is a crucial part of the process. So is knowing how to connect an idea to your audience's most pressing concerns and interests. Persuasion, like knowledge, is inherently social.

2
Learning

In times of drastic change, it is the learners who inherit the future. The learned usually find themselves beautifully equipped to live in a world that no longer exists.
—Eric Hoffer, *Reflections on the Human Condition*

When Ed established NASA's project academy in the 1990s, he arranged for it to have a permanent residential home at the agency's Wallops Flight Facility on Wallops Island, Virginia. The island has hosted a government rocket testing site since the end of World War II. The ability to convene emerging leaders from NASA's various centers in a remote location helped to make the program a bonding experience that took participants out of the silos of their respective home organizations. The dormitories and dining hall at Wallops had the look and feel of a summer camp from a bygone era. Each building had a rack of bicycles out front that were freely available for riding around the base. The conversations and arguments that began during long days in the classroom continued over long evenings in the cafeteria and the bar.

The subject of the arguments one year was NASA administrator Dan Goldin's management philosophy: "Faster, Better, Cheaper."[1] When Goldin arrived at the agency in 1992, NASA was coming off a terrible stretch that included the loss of the space shuttle *Challenger* and its crew and the launch of the Hubble Space Telescope with a significant flaw in its primary mirror. Goldin was determined to whip the agency into shape, and he took the development of its technical workforce seriously. He would fly from NASA headquarters in Washington, DC, to Wallops for an evening to address each cohort of the project management training program. Goldin's talks always generated heated discussions that went on late into the night.

In anticipation of Goldin's visit, the participants objected that "Faster, Better, Cheaper" simply wasn't feasible at NASA. The policy guidelines and project controls were too onerous. There were too many meetings. The bureaucracy was impenetrable. General Jack Dailey, a retired Marine Corps assistant commandant who served as Goldin's associate deputy administrator, got word of the class's objections and told Ed he was willing to come down and give the students a fair hearing as long as they were ready to show up with solutions rather than complaints.

After a particularly contentious classroom discussion with one of Ed's instructors, Ed told the students that they would have an opportunity to voice their concerns directly to NASA's senior leadership: "Jack Dailey has agreed to come and talk with you if you're ready to have a real dialogue." The class went silent for a moment. They began to discuss the pros and cons of telling the unvarnished truth. Some said yes, others said no. Some were afraid of consequences for their careers. Others worried that their reward for speaking up would be getting pulled off flight projects and staffed on bureaucratic change management initiatives after the course ended. But eventually they agreed to a meeting in a week.

Now they had to work as a team to present a unified, coherent argument to a key decision maker, and they couldn't agree on anything.

Ed identified a quiet woman in the male-dominated class as an ideal leader for this opportunity. He could tell that her classmates respected her, and that her calm temperament might be just what was needed to get this noisy group of men to listen to one another. "You should lead this," Ed told her privately, much to her surprise. She rose to the challenge.

In the end, the team came together and made recommendations that would allow new flexibilities within NASA's project management procedures document. Their presentation received an open-minded hearing from Dailey. Some of the class continued working on these issues after the course ended. The outcomes were not perfect—like many course corrections, these created new unanticipated problems—but the participants had the experience of learning as a team to address an objective that had value and meaning at the highest levels of the organization.

The class's experience spoke to a truism that is seldom acknowledged. Learning is uncomfortable, particularly when the status quo has been disrupted. Goldin had confronted NASA with a challenge: change or die. Every organization eventually reaches that inflection point. What happens when the behaviors, processes, and methods that once promoted success now lead to stagnation or failure? Who is responsible for delivering an organizational response that ensures continuous learning and development?

Learning on Three Levels

Learning in a professional setting is not an isolated activity. It takes place within a broader context that requires action. The starting point for learning is an experience or problem. This experience leads to reflection on what is happening, followed by the development of an abstract hypothesis to address the experience or problem. The final step is action through experimentation, which leads to new experiences, creating a cycle. Without experience, learning becomes a series of disconnected abstract concepts.[2]

Learning often meets resistance because it demands changes in mindset, skill, and performance. These changes can be difficult and even painful, and as a result they elicit strong emotions. The emotional dimension of learning generally receives little attention unless it falls under the banner of "change management," but learning is always more than a purely cognitive experience.

The word *learning* often leads to thoughts of *training*. We have always thought this was a poor synonym for learning, since training is often thought of as something you do with a dog. Training traditionally implies a classroom exercise where a fellow employee or a consultant teaches the processes, routines, technologies, or expected behaviors of the organization. In recent years much of this work has migrated to online courses, but the substance hasn't changed significantly. The main faults with this model in a project context are threefold: these activities rarely reflect the way employees actually learn, there is little room for substantive discussion and feedback, and there is almost no integration with the learning done at other levels in the organization. Very few employees have warm feelings toward training, and many say its primary value is in meeting colleagues and sharing stories with them.

The simple fact is that most people overwhelmingly learn from one another on the job, and what they learn from formal training is rarely critical and often irrelevant.[3] Fortunately, training represents just one of many ways to learn in a professional setting. Rotational assignments, hands-on opportunities, problem challenges and contests (e.g., hackathons), storytelling forums, and partnership programs with universities can all provide valuable learning experiences for individuals.

Team learning generally receives far less attention than learning at the individual level. The agile movement has recentered attention on the primacy of teams in project performance, and it recognizes the importance of face-to-face conversations and the need for regular opportunities for team reflection. Beyond agile initiatives, dedicated efforts to promote team learning tend to be sporadic. Sometimes teams set aside a day for a retreat, and occasionally a group's efforts result in lessons learned or case studies that can be used by others. In project-based organizations that haven't adopted agile methods, there are rarely more formal approaches unless regulatory or safety issues come into play, such as in the nuclear power industry. Because project teams are often temporary, their learning frequently gets passed on as stories that become part of the firm's learning repertoire and culture.

Rarer still is learning at the organizational level. This raises a legitimate question: is it even possible for an organization to learn? The concept of organizational learning (and related concepts such as collective intelligence) is based on the idea that in a group of employees, partners, and stakeholders, there is ample knowledge to solve problems. But how exactly does this happen, and who is accountable for the desired outcomes? Katie Smith Milway and Amy Saxton identify three challenges to organizational learning: lack of clarity around measures of organizational knowledge and related outcomes, poor incentives for learning, and uncertainty about the best ways to create and transfer knowledge across an organization.[4]

Occasionally firms undertake enterprise-wide learning when facing an existential threat or systemic challenge. (Chipotle and Starbucks are recent high-profile examples: Chipotle retrained all its employees in response to repeated outbreaks of food poisoning, and Starbucks sought to address issues related to racial bias.[5]) Sometimes initiatives such as the wholesale adoption of agile or lean methodologies permeate an entire organization, but this kind of activity typically starts within an engineering, operations, or information technology unit and then gains executive buy-in and sponsorship. Even in these cases, learning is not usually identified as an organizational outcome since agile transformation typically focuses on the level of product or service delivery. Although organization-wide learning may not always be necessary or feasible, the organization still has a critical role to fulfill: to facilitate learning when and where it's needed.

While individual learning gets the lion's share of attention, savvy organizations have recognized the value in approaching learning as an integrated effort that happens at all three levels:

Organizational—promoting sustainable performance and innovation

Team—enabling project success

Individual—building competence, capability, and confidence

This enables senior management to better understand the culture of the organization and to identify steps to change it where necessary. Leaders can evaluate the social infrastructure of the organization and look for opportunities to integrate learning into the ways their employees actually work. Teams can gain access to outside knowledge and guidance as well as the ability to learn directly from more experienced members of the organization. And all employees can have the experience of learning—not through training—the story of the organization, its values and strategies, and, most importantly, the connection between their roles and the organization's ability to execute its mission.

Organizational Learning

The day after the space shuttle *Columbia* lifted off from Kennedy Space Center on January 16, 2003, to begin shuttle mission STS-107, analysts reviewing high-speed photography of the launch noticed that the leading edge of *Columbia*'s left wing had been damaged by debris that flew off the shuttle's external fuel tank 81.7 seconds after launch. While the astronauts aboard *Columbia* busily executed their mission in space over the coming days, team members on the ground worked hard to determine the extent of the damage to the shuttle and its likely consequences. Communication with the shuttle crew minimized concerns about the debris strike to the wing, suggesting it would be a routine maintenance issue once *Columbia* returned to Earth. Although some engineers expressed significant concerns about the damage, the mission management team concluded that it was not a "safety-of-flight issue."[6] On February 1, 2003, as the shuttle reentered Earth's atmosphere, the heat generated by reentry overwhelmed the damaged spacecraft. Within moments the shuttle broke apart, killing the crew.

The aftermath of *Columbia* set off a reckoning within NASA. The accident investigation report pointed to learning that should have happened after the 1986 *Challenger* accident but hadn't. This learning primarily concerned organizational behavior, not technical know-how. Employees "normalized" persistent technical problems before both accidents, which led them to minimize risks that had potentially catastrophic consequences. Many were reluctant to speak up when they thought something was wrong, and when technical experts did speak up, managers overruled or simply ignored them. The agency hadn't taught its people the lessons of *Challenger*, explicitly or otherwise.

This changed in the post-*Columbia* era. In addition to revamping its governance model and establishing a formal process to protect dissenting opinions, NASA established strategies to ensure that agency-wide knowledge and learning were in good shape. As leader of its project academy, Ed now reported to the organization's chief engineer, who reported to the NASA administrator, the agency's presidentially appointed leader. This simple structural design ensured tight connections to both senior leadership and the technical workforce.

One factor that kept knowledge and learning activities visible at the executive level was quarterly reviews by the agency's Program Management Council, one of NASA's top three governing bodies. These were formal scheduled meetings to review performance, problems, and opportunities, just like regular executive reviews of major space flight programs or projects. These meetings ensured that learning was aligned with organizational strategies and mission performance. The visibility of these meetings had the additional benefit of communicating to the entire workforce the seriousness of learning and knowledge.

This experience points to a central requirement for successful learning and knowledge systems: they have to be closely aligned with and managed by senior leadership. They cannot operate as an HR function that's disconnected from corporate strategy. Leadership sponsorship and engagement are essential. At NASA's academy, leaders from engineering, project management, safety, business, and science were responsible for identifying critical capabilities, designing learning events, and serving as faculty. At such educational events, senior executives would be exposed to conversations about the practitioners' reality—both the good and the bad. Many NASA policies and standards were formulated and designed through engagements like these between executive leaders and practitioners. More to the point, the vast majority of senior leaders went through the same learning their workforce experienced. Communities and networks of learning crossed the spectrum of NASA.

An organization uses a combination of signals and incentives to send a message about the value of learning. At a high level, organizational efforts generally boil down to 1) investments in learning infrastructure, and 2) reinforcement through culture.

Significant investments in learning infrastructure are a sign that management has skin in the game, though dollars are nowhere near as important as a savvy approach that aligns with the organization's strategy and way of working. Overinvestment in technology-based solutions or poorly designed training can backfire, leading to frustration and poor morale. The primary dimensions of learning infrastructure include *integration, resources, time and space,* and *networks.*

Integration. An integrated approach to learning often comes from the establishment of a learning or knowledge office. Many organizations now appoint a chief learning officer or chief knowledge officer, but the title matters less than support from senior leadership, a clear and necessary connection to business strategy, and credibility with the organization's practitioners. It cannot be emphasized enough that organizational learning must be focused on meeting the strategic needs of leaders and the tactical needs of practitioners. Too often, the disciplines that fall under learning (e.g., organization development, knowledge management, process management, or innovation) become parochial and focused on developments in their fields as opposed to the organization they serve. Leadership- and practitioner-centric approaches are necessary to assure that learning enables individuals and teams to find *a* best way, and not *the* best way.

When Ed first established NASA's project academy, its bureaucratic home was within the agency's vast human resources function, which did not speak highly of its standing in an organization that prizes engineering excellence. When he had the opportunity to move the project academy to the Office of the Chief Engineer and fold engineering leadership development into the academy's mission, the proximity to the chief engineer sent a message to the technical workforce about the value of learning. Several years later, when NASA's leadership asked Ed to become the first chief knowledge officer, he insisted on remaining within the engineering organization rather than moving to the administrator's office in order to maintain the hard-earned credibility with practitioners that had taken years to establish. (See chapter 1 for more about this.) And, as mentioned previously, quarterly reviews of the learning and knowledge systems by senior management strengthened integration and ensured the alignment of learning with organizational strategy.

Resources. Learning infrastructure can include physical or digital assets such as research libraries, databases, publications, and expert networks. For global consulting firms, the ability of employees to learn rapidly is critical to successful client service. McKinsey, a privately held partnership, is known to spend a double-digit percentage of its revenue on knowledge and learning.[7] Large investment firms spend prolifically on sell-side research, direct access to experts, and subscriptions to journals and newsletters, and law firms make similar kinds of expenditures.

Time and space. In a world where time is increasingly synonymous with money, organizations can incentivize learning by giving people time to learn. Google's 20% Project, which encouraged engineers to spend one-fifth of their time on personal projects, led to breakthrough products like Gmail and AdSense. Time can also be earmarked for participating in conferences, seminars, classes, or Maker Faires. And as detailed in chapter 1, spaces—physical or otherwise—play an important part in learning. Hosting an organization-wide event such as a hackathon is an example of creating a space for learning.

Networks. Every firm is inherently filled with networks of knowledge and know-how. "There's a bit of 'I know,' and there's a lot more of 'I know who knows it,'" says Ray Ryan of Square.[8] The challenge at the organizational level is in enabling people to connect as seamlessly as possible to learn from others and share what they know. Larry's research into knowledge networks with Katrina Pugh identified four distinct goals that these networks can have: coordination, learning/innovation, translation/local adaptation, and support of individual members.[9] Given the range of these goals, there's no single best way for an organization to develop and leverage networks. Successful networks reflect culture and a shared sense of mission. McKinsey's thousands of consultants around the globe are expected to return a call from any other consultant in the company within 24 hours.[10] Experience with this kind of responsiveness in a network fosters a strong sense of reciprocity.

Ed found that some of NASA's most successful networks used different incentives to encourage participation. The NASA Engineering & Safety Center (NESC), established in the wake of the *Columbia* accident, selected top engineers from each NASA center to serve as members of an elite network that would provide independent assessments of programs and projects facing technical challenges. The founder of the NESC gained buy-in on the supply side by recognizing the experts and inviting them to join without leaving their day jobs, and on the demand side by offering the network's services only when requested. The network thrived because there was no top-down pressure associated with it.

A learning organization also invests in outside networks that broaden its reach and capacity. These can range from memberships in professional associations (e.g., IEEE for electrical engineers or the American Medical Association for doctors) to commercial expert networks such as Gerson Lehrman Group (GLG), which offers on-demand access to hundreds of thousands of experts in a wide range of industries, sectors, and geographies. Some of these networks are entirely remote and asynchronous. Software developers of all ages around the globe rely on Stack Overflow, a network of 10 million registered users who troubleshoot problems and share solutions with each other. Learning is increasingly an outside-in opportunity.

When some people think of knowledge networks, the first examples that spring to mind are communities of practice or interest. Larry uses a simple analogy to distinguish between a network and a community. The alumni of an elite university are part of a network: they are all connected, but they don't know each other. Communities are smaller and more personal—people know and care about each other. Communities of practice or interest can be extraordinarily valuable, but they're narrower in scope than networks. Communities can be seeded at the organizational level, but they quickly become ghost towns if they don't have a constituency that keeps them alive.

Infrastructure can only take an organization so far. The presence of a learning culture is the real indication that learning matters. It's one thing to own exercise equipment, but it's another to use it every day as a matter of habit. Some of the hallmarks of a learning culture include *recognition, leadership support and participation, iterative experimentation, unlearning* behaviors that have impeded learning, and *connection*.

Recognition. Firms can recognize the value of learning in multiple ways. Do executives with a demonstrated commitment to learning get the top jobs? After NASA's project academy helped to develop a decade's worth of emerging leaders, some of those alumni began to rise into top positions within the agency. In 2004, NASA's new administrator appointed a project academy alumnus as NASA's chief engineer, then quickly promoted him to serve as the top civil servant within the agency. The chief engineer who replaced him was also a project academy alumnus and advocate. This recognition of leaders who valued learning sent a signal about NASA's priorities as it recovered from the loss of *Columbia* and prepared to undertake a new human space flight mission.

Organizations can also recognize learning through events that explicitly acknowledge and even celebrate the importance of getting things wrong. Athough "fail fast" has been a Silicon Valley mantra for decades, there's more to it than speed; failure without reflection is a recipe for perfecting the same mistakes. The World Bank has hosted FAILfaires (failure fairs) to share lessons about approaches that haven't worked.[11] By letting people know that failure is an expected part of the learning process, organizations can encourage healthy dialogue rather than incentivizing people to hide their failures. The World Bank is not alone among large organizations in adopting this approach; other organizations, including the Gates Foundation, have held failure festivals. Ronald Bledlow of Singapore Management University has found that the failure stories of others can motivate learning in a way that success stories do not: "People may actually learn more and retain a more elaborate memory of other people's failures as compared to their successes."[12]

Leadership support and participation. A learning culture requires support and advocacy from the top of the organization. Do leaders participate in events that demonstrate their own commitment to learning? The first generation of NASA's project academy emphasized leaders as teachers: the project management training courses were taught by senior project managers. In later years, senior leaders would regularly take part in the annual agency-wide project management conference in order to share strategic insights with experienced practitioners.

Plenty of other organizations have leaders whose actions speak to the value of learning. Former HBO CEO Richard Plepler would spend a few hours speaking with each small cohort chosen for the company's Directors Leadership Program, which groomed emerging executives one level below vice presidents. Leaders such as Reid Hoffman of LinkedIn or Brad Smith of Microsoft demonstrate thought leadership by writing books that address substantive challenges in their fields. (These should not be confused with ghostwritten CEO success stories.) Others host conversations, podcasts, or book clubs, or find other novel ways to share new ideas. When leaders make clear that learning matters, it can set a tone throughout an organization.

These behaviors can help contribute to a sense of psychological safety—a shared sense that a team is safe to take risks such as introducing new ideas or providing critical feedback. The evidence pointing to the importance of psychological safety is well validated in a variety of sectors and organizations. (See the "Team Learning" section below and chapter 5 for more on this.) Psychological safety is oxygen for a learning organization; it's impossible to imagine one without it. At firms like Bridgewater Associates, which practices a kind of radical transparency that's uncommon in most corporate settings, the focus is on building a culture where mistakes are aired rather than airbrushed.

Iterative experimentation. Organizations, like the people within them, learn by doing. Before rolling out top-down company-wide initiatives, experienced leaders in learning organizations run experiments to figure out what works best in a given context. In short, they think big and start small. At NASA, Ed ran initial knowledge-sharing events and publications as pilot programs, and only established knowledge sharing as a formal business line of the project academy once the offerings were relatively mature. For example, after putting out a series of papers called "Issues in NASA Program and Project Management," which experimented with first-person narratives, he then started *ASK Magazine*, a publication that focused primarily on practitioner stories. This approach allowed him to try new ideas and make adjustments without facing the expectations of a formal program rollout. Particularly in situations involving technology, limited test runs with small groups of practitioners can save countless time, money, and frustration.

In agile teams, experimentation is vital to increasing speed, improving quality, and lessening the impact of failure. Small, early failures are easy to handle, and provide opportunities to learn and improve.

Experimentation is likely to become a more rigorous process in the future. Much experimentation today is of the trial-and-error variety, but sophisticated organizations see experimentation as an opportunity to test hypotheses based on probabilities rather than hunches and to glean insights from data. The highest-performing organizations of the decade ahead will rely more on science than guesswork.[13]

Unlearning. In order for an organization to shift direction and adopt a learning posture, the people within the organization have to unlearn behaviors and habits that have held the organization back in the past. For example, if people have guarded knowledge rather than shared it or elevated team loyalty over transparency with the broader organization, these norms have to change to create space for learning to happen. As Edgar Schein has noted, learning anxiety—the fear of trying something new—can only be overcome by either a greater survival anxiety (e.g., the prospect of job loss for failing to adapt) or an increase in psychological safety that reduces the resistance to change.[14] Again, leaders who model new behaviors signal that it's safe to lower existing barriers.

A novel approach to unlearning is the Friction Project, an initiative by Stanford professors Bob Sutton and Huggy Rao that seeks to "understand the causes and cures for destructive organizational friction."[15] It has studied firms such as AstraZeneca, which made an organization-wide commitment to simplification in order to free up hundreds of thousands of wasted hours that could be put to more constructive uses. AstraZeneca asked its employees to identify their own sources of friction and propose plans to reduce it. At AstraZeneca China, for example, its sales professionals found ways to reduce paperwork and simplify tools and processes, saving 1.7 hours per week per sales rep, which added up to $600,000 in lost time per year.[16]

Connection. Where learning is concerned, connection must come before content. A key aspect of our colleague Nancy Dixon's life-long work is research that underscores the need for relationships, trust, and connection.[17] Once the question "Who is this?" has been answered, then people can focus on "What are they saying?" When Ed convened NASA's knowledge community for the first time after having been named the agency's chief knowledge officer, he arranged the meeting in a circle to promote participation, interaction, and collegiality. Seeing people's eyes is an important part of engagement. Once people settled into their seats, NASA chief engineer Michael Ryschkewitsch opened the meeting by explaining the importance of this effort for NASA and its future mission. That opening retreat created the connections that would promote the early success of the team.

Team Learning

At the beginning of the COVID-19 global pandemic, the United States and other nations faced critical shortages of ventilators. Senior leaders at the Jet Propulsion Laboratory quickly decided to convene a project that could help address this need by designing a prototype for a ventilator that could be assembled using commercial off-the-shelf parts.[18]

When the VITAL (Ventilator Intervention Technology Accessible Locally) team held its kickoff meeting on March 16, 2020, none of its team members were experts in the development of medical devices. David Van Buren, creator of the project, had set out to assemble a Jet Propulsion Laboratory (JPL) team with diversity in age, gender, and race. "He was looking for people who were proactive, creative, resourceful, flexible, rigorous, and forceful but kind," says Carey Weisberg, an optical engineer who served as executive assistant to the VITAL leadership team.[19] They knew the learning curve ahead was steep. "Be comfortable being ignorant (at least until you're not)" was a guiding principle from the start.

That two-hour kickoff meeting was a crash course in the subject matter. Michael Gurevitch, a pulmonologist at Huntington Memorial Hospital, gave the team a brief biology lesson about viruses, followed by a detailed description of ventilators. He brought a ventilator as a visual aid. As he spoke, Sarah Hovsepian, who later became the team's test coordination and verification & validation lead, furiously scribbled notes on a white board. The headings she identified on the board—machine parameters, mandatory features, safety requirements/machine outputs, key requirements (medical, operational, unknown), and questions—became the first-draft requirements for the ventilator.

Some of the earliest learning happened through self-directed online study to fill basic knowledge gaps. Team members also tapped their personal networks. "I talked to my sister who is a nurse practitioner/hospitalist and asked questions of ICU workers and intensivists in her network," said Stacey Boland, operations team lead. "VITAL was so fast that we had to get out of our comfort zones and just call people sometimes."

Starting from US and UK government regulations for ventilators approved for emergency use, the VITAL team continued developing the requirements, relying on a handful of physicians and medical device industry contacts for rapid feedback. The team was then able to review its draft requirements with a larger "community of interest" that included medical clinicians, FDA representatives, manufacturers of ventilators and other related devices, and the team's own broader engineering community. "A key aspect was actually continuing to listen to the clinicians as they discussed the design and eventually the as-tested function of the devices," says Brett Kennedy, requirement lead. The team practiced "radical transparency" and open editing of the requirements and other project materials. The use of Google Suite enabled simultaneous real-time collaboration on documents. Even under the tightest of timelines, the team understood the importance of learning and knowledge sharing. As the project transitioned to licensing the device, its sub-teams such as design, operations, and production recorded meetings to capture lessons learned. After just 37 days, the VITAL team's efforts led to the delivery of a prototype ventilator that passed acceptance tests performed by Mt. Sinai Hospital in New York, a staggering feat of team learning.

In our experience, organizations often overlook the value of team learning. NASA made a significant effort to invest in team learning only after a fateful flight that Ed took with NASA's then-administrator Dan Goldin at the end of the 1990s. NASA had just experienced two high-profile flops in its Mars program—the Mars Climate Orbiter and Mars Polar Lander failed within a few months of each other. On this flight, Ed sat across from his boss on a tiny plane headed to the agency's management training facility on Wallops Island in southern Virginia. Ed could tell he was in trouble: the administrator refused to talk to him or even look at him. Finally, Goldin exploded in rage, making it clear that he held Ed's project academy responsible for not providing support to NASA's project teams that might have helped prevent the Mars failures. Ed recognized a truth in that tongue-lashing, and he set out to find the most effective ways to promote team learning in the NASA context.

Efforts to promote team learning should consider big-picture issues like *project relevance*, cultural factors that promote *safety to challenge the status quo*, and resources such as *space and time* and *targeted support*.

Project relevance. Any consideration of team learning has to begin with a recognition that the team's mission or objective is valued by the organization. In the midst of an emerging global crisis, the VITAL team had the support of the leaders of the Jet Propulsion Laboratory and NASA.

At the other extreme, an ad hoc team assembled to promote a hastily approved change initiative that's not supported by senior leadership stands little chance of learning to enhance its performance. This may sound obvious, but anyone who has worked in a large, bureaucratic organization has probably witnessed a team that was doomed to fail before its kickoff meeting. There can be any number of reasons for this, from ill-conceived ideas to political naivete, but the end result is always the same if a team's mission is not respected by the organization's leaders.

Safety to challenge the status quo. More than a decade after Amy Edmondson of Harvard Business School and her colleagues conducted research among teams peforming cardiac surgery and identified psychological safety as vital to team learning,[20] Google came to a similar conclusion when it crunched the numbers on teams within its organization. It found that psychological safety—not skills, personality type, or background—was the key attribute of its most effective teams.[21] Specific behaviors like turn-taking in conversations and listening were common among its best teams, showing that empathy played a measurable role in team performance. NASA's support for project teams employed pre- and post-intervention surveys of team members to gauge changes in feelings of openness and trust, which are critical to fostering a healthy team context.

Chris Argyris, one of the most influential theorists of organizational development, argued for a different characteristic of learning teams and organizations, which he dubbed "double-loop" learning.[22]

This is what happens when teams go beyond learning that simply addresses a problem with a linear solution (single-loop learning) and respond instead by delving deeply into context and questioning the underlying values, beliefs, and norms that frame the problem. Seen from this vantage point, project reviews are places for argument, exchange, and exploration, and risk management is a tool for learning to understand the likelihood of failure.

Space and time. The greatest barriers to learning at any level are simply space and time. A significant weakness of the project age is the schedule pressures placed on teams. The pressure to make decisions, experiment, and implement can instill a reluctance to spend time on learning, conversation, and reflection.

At the team level, spaces for discussion, bonding, and knowledge sharing can take multiple forms. Meetings are the primary venue, but routinely scheduled meetings can become formulaic to the point where people say only what's absolutely necessary in order to get through the meeting as quickly as possible. Creating space for dialogue requires intention. From after-action events to offsite retreats, there are myriad approaches a team can take. The real currency at stake is time to learn.

Technology can create a space for team learning, particularly when it allows for asynchronous conversations on distributed teams working across time zones. The ability of team members to ask each other questions through a Slack channel, for instance, can close distances between remote or virtual teams. The ability to monitor multiple ongoing conversations on Slack provides opportunities for learning that aren't possible with live dialogues.[23]

Targeted support. When a project team goes off-course, a well-planned intervention can unblock channels that have inhibited learning and knowledge sharing. NASA's project academy supported teams by providing assessments, workshops, and follow-on coaching for teams and their individual members. The facilitators and coaches were primarily NASA veterans who knew the organization and its culture. These workshops focused on cultivating the attitudes and behaviors found on high-performing teams, such as practicing appreciation and inclusion, keeping commitments to team members, and eliminating toxic attitudes and behaviors.

Individual Learning

As noted at the beginning of this chapter, there's ample evidence that most individual learning takes place on the job. But in the words of James March of Stanford Business School, "Experience may possibly be the best teacher, but it is not a particularly good teacher."[24]

The context for individual learning has evolved as a result of technology. T. K. Mattingly, one of only two astronauts to fly to the moon and on the space shuttle, observed a fundamental difference in the way Apollo-era engineers and later generations at NASA learned their trade. Before the IT revolution made coding and calculation machine tasks, engineers knew their data intimately because of literal hands-on experience with them. As powerful software tools took over this work, the process by which individuals developed engineering judgment changed.[25] The implications of this are unclear, but it points to the challenge of understanding how individuals gain expertise as "symbolic analysts" rather than craftsmen.[26]

Ed's approach through NASA's project academy was to build competence, capability, and confidence. If competence is about possessing specific knowledge and skills, capability speaks more broadly to knowing how to learn from experience. Confidence grows over time as a byproduct of personal development and validation from teammates.

Given the limitations of traditional training and the centrality of teamwork in projects, the NASA project academy looked for innovative ways to develop individual talent. In 2008 it introduced Project HOPE (Hands-On Project Experience), a learning opportunity in which a group of young professionals would work as a project team on a flight project from start to finish. HOPE projects offered a chance to get intensive hands-on experience with flight hardware as well as mentoring and coaching support, and they provided time and space for participants to reflect on lessons from their experience.[27] Learning was the first goal of HOPE, followed closely by actual mission success.

Rotational assignments present another way of building individual capability. While some large firms put young professionals through a series of rotational assignments to expose them to the breadth of the firm's functions early in their careers before they settle into a primary role, LinkedIn took an approach that looked like this on the surface and fundamentally reshaped it.[28] Adapting a concept from the US military, it characterized individual assignments as "tours of duty" to accomplish a specific mission over a period of a few years. It went further and categorized different types of tours of duty. In addition to rotational tours, which are similar to those described above, it identified transformational tours, in which an individual has the opportunity to develop significant capability to deliver results, and foundational tours, which build increasing alignment between the individual and the firm. The tour-of-duty model is consistent with the experience of professionals in project-based organizations who gain increasing levels of expertise and responsibility as they move from project to project.

What ultimately makes individuals effective in a project organization? At a series of NASA knowledge-sharing events from 2007 to 2009, Ed asked 275 senior practitioners a simple question: "How do you learn to do your job?" These practitioners, mostly project managers and systems engineers, discussed this in groups of six to eight and wrote up their responses on flip charts. Some groups made diagrams, others came up with lists, and still others drew detailed pictures. Ed and Matt collated these responses and ultimately identified four key dimensions of effectiveness:

Ability—a combination of natural aptitude and the capability to incorporate new knowledge and learn from experience.

Attitude—motivation, curiosity, a growth mindset, and the willingness to work as a member of a team.

Assignments—core on-the-job learning experiences that lead to personal development.

Alliances—relationships that enable an individual to succeed within the organization.

These "4 A's" provide a lens for thinking about individual development as a process that is both personal and social. Ability and attitude are personal qualities, while alliances and assignments are both rooted in relationships with others.

Long before the 4 A's exercise, NASA's project academy began by focusing on developing individual project management talent. The foundation of these efforts was the establishment of a competency model for project management. The model included a range of knowledge and skills from cost estimating to stakeholder management that was deemed necessary to manage NASA projects successfully. The initial inputs came from extensive in-depth interviews with senior NASA project managers and systems engineers. After working through curriculum development methodologies and holding practitioner focus groups, the academy vetted its draft competency model with both internal and external organizations. At a large bureaucracy like NASA, this also meant aligning the competency model with existing policies and procedures as well as homegrown competency models at NASA's centers. The result formed the basis for both a curriculum and a career development model for project managers. In the decades since the initial competency model, NASA has made periodic updates to keep up with changes in project management, technology, and developments such as new Office of Management and Budget requirements for federal government project managers.

While competency models are important, they speak more to abilities than attitude. "For learning from experience to be effective, the learner must be self-aware and have a degree of humility," writes Lynn Crawford of the University of Sydney about the development of managers of complex projects.[29] The so-called soft skills of project management remain the most underappreciated tools in individual development: they open the door for continuous learning.

Putting Learning to Work

What can organizations do to promote learning at all levels? Here are some suggestions.

Promote leaders as teachers, which contributes in many ways to the value of learning. Under Ed's leadership, the NASA project academy always invited executives, engineers, and scientists to present at events ranging from training courses and knowledge forums to conferences. These speakers believed they were there to teach, but they also learned from and connected with practitioners. The visibility of having leaders as teachers signals to the workforce that learning matters.

Establish reflective leadership as a clear goal. In the NASA project academy's strategy for knowledge sharing, creating more reflective leaders and practitioners was the first goal. This was really about convincing people that reflection was an activity worthy of their most treasured resource: time. A documented and verbalized commitment to reflective leadership should clearly indicate that there is a responsibility for each practitioner and leader to take time for reflection and learning.

Approach training as a conversation that makes productive use of argument and dissent. Training often turns off smart people. Asking people to share their own experiences and perspective gives them a voice and helps to foster inclusion and appreciation.

Create spaces and places where learning takes place. NASA provided many places where people would come together for the purpose of learning, sharing, and growing. In recent years, young professionals at NASA have solicited leadership support to establish workspaces that enable co-creation, collaboration, sharing, and networking.[30]

Learn in small gatherings and communities. When people learn together, they get better at working together. This goes beyond intelligence to social capital. Spending significant time together in a learning environment will lead to profound work relationships for life if the event has been designed correctly. This includes providing opportunities for eating, drinking, and socializing together.

Learning is not overhead. It is the ultimate competitive advantage for every leader, team, and organization. The best teams and organizations clearly articulate the requirement for learning, reflection, and knowledge sharing as part of mission strategy and success. What NASA has done well is to create expectations, requirements, policies, executive sponsorship, and resources for exceptional learning opportunities. Learning is not a "nice-to-have" perk that can be cut when funding becomes tight.

A diversity of voices is vital. One of the first principles for the NASA project academy was to offer *a* way, not *the* way, to enable project success. When learning is shared from a variety of perspectives, people understand that they are free to accept, question, improve on, or tailor for their own context. Psychological safety reassures them that all voices are welcome.

3

Stories: Knowledge, Meaning, and Community

Storytelling reveals meaning without committing the error of defining it.

—Hannah Arendt, *Men in Dark Times*

It was a brisk 36 degrees on January 28, 1986, at the Kennedy Space Center in Florida as NASA's launch team began the final countdown to send the space shuttle *Challenger* into orbit at 11:38 a.m. The launch had been scheduled for the previous day, but it was scrubbed due to high winds. *Challenger*'s crew of seven included Christa McAuliffe, a schoolteacher from New Hampshire who had been selected to serve as the first citizen passenger on a space shuttle mission. Interest in the McAuliffe story had led to a huge wave of publicity, with CNN providing live coverage of the flight. Seventy-three seconds after launch, the shuttle burst into flames, killing the crew instantly and leaving a trail of white vapor that disintegrated slowly into the blue sky. That indelible image shocked a nation accustomed to routine success from its space program. The *Challenger* accident and its aftermath shook NASA to its core.

The failure of a seal on *Challenger*'s solid rocket boosters, which initiated a sudden series of events resulting in the loss of the shuttle and its crew, did not surprise engineers who had cautioned NASA officials just a day earlier against launching at such cold temperatures. Several previous shuttle flights had experienced problems with the solid rocket booster's O-rings failing to seal properly. The night before the launch, Roger Boisjoly, an engineer at Morton Thiokol, the manufacturer of the solid rocket boosters, had argued forcefully in telephone meetings with leaders from NASA and his own company against launching at temperatures below 53 degrees. Boisjoly had written a memo six months earlier warning of the consequences of an O-ring failure: "The result would be a catastrophe of the highest order—loss of human life."[1]

The *Challenger* disaster proved to be a pivotal moment for NASA. The stunning success of Apollo was replaced with a new story: NASA had gone from an elite organization that could do the impossible to a routine one plagued by bureaucracy.

The Presidential Commission on the Space Shuttle Challenger Accident (also known as the Rogers Commission) blasted NASA and outlined major recommendations for the agency before a return to flight. NASA's leadership responded by committing to significant actions. Phil Culbertson, a senior NASA executive, said, "We're going to reexamine our management thoroughly . . . and I suspect we will make some fundamental changes."[2] But the changes demanded by the commission and implemented by NASA did not fully address the problems that *Challenger* had exposed. In addition to technical and structural reforms, the commission called for NASA to develop plans and policies for "the implementation of effective management communications at all levels," a recommendation so vague as to be meaningless. It cited a tendency at Marshall Space Flight Center, the home of the space shuttle's solid rocket booster program, for "management isolation," but that was it. The words *culture* and *learning* (in the organizational sense) did not appear anywhere in the Rogers Commission report.[3]

These were critical omissions because the culture that led to the *Challenger* accident was one in which employees might be reluctant to speak up if they sensed that something was wrong. Allan McDonald, a Morton Thiokol official who had refused to go along with his management's decision to confirm in writing for NASA that it would be safe to launch *Challenger* into freezing temperatures, recounted intimidating remarks made in the teleconferences the night before the launch.[4] McDonald had stood his ground in the face of tremendous pressure, but his account spoke to a lack of psychological safety that needed to be addressed. An organization that disregarded the advice of its technical experts had to change more than its management structure. It had to come to grips with the human dimension of this difficult story and learn from it.

NASA did not learn from *Challenger* right away. As business schools wrote case studies about it, NASA hesitated to develop its own case study because the loss hit too close to home. But the accident opened the door for project management learning that eventually led to a concerted effort to harness the power of stories.

A Need to Learn Differently

What NASA experienced in the mid-1980s was a failure to listen, learn, and adapt to a changing world. *Challenger* was the agency's most visible and deadly disaster of the era, but it was not its only one.[5] In the wake of the *Challenger* investigation, and despite pressure to reform the way it managed its programs and projects, NASA continued to experience serious setbacks as a result of its failure to learn. The agency's next launch, a Delta rocket carrying a government weather satellite, failed in May 1986. Ten months later, NASA lost yet another launch vehicle tasked with lifting a Department of Defense satellite into orbit. The pressure created by these incidents would open the door to learning and new ways of working, but it would take more than a decade and the loss of the space shuttle *Columbia* for the generation that grew up during the *Challenger* fallout to assume leadership positions and fully implement its most intangible lessons around communication and culture.

NASA's difficulties during the *Challenger* period stemmed in part from broad changes in the way the agency did its work.[6] A generation earlier, during the era of the Apollo moon landings, NASA had relied on an informal apprentice model to develop skills and transfer knowledge from one person to another. There had been myriad opportunities for on-the-job learning early in a career; the average age of an Apollo 11 flight controller was 28 years old.[7] Engineers and technicians had done much of the math for Apollo by hand, with no tools other than a slide rule. This labor-intensive approach had helped to instill a sense of engineering judgment that came from being close to the numbers. But by the 1980s, work became increasingly specialized. Subject experts were separated by discipline and often by location. Absent a clearly defined unifying mission like Apollo, silos emerged between civil servants and contractors as well as among NASA's different centers across the country.

A new way of working, triggered by exponential growth in computing power, a revolution in software, and the widespread use of personal computers, hastened a tremendous growth of specialist knowledge that made projects far more complex than they had been a generation earlier. George Low, a leader of the Apollo program, notes that only 100 wires had linked the Saturn rocket to the Apollo spacecraft: "A single man can fully understand this interface and can cope with all the effects of a change on either side of the interface. If there had been 10 times as many wires, it probably would have taken a hundred (or a thousand?) times as many people to handle the interface."[8] The growth of information technology brought tremendous benefits and efficiencies to NASA, but it also short-circuited the apprentice model that had shaped the earlier generation of employees. There were fewer opportunities for hands-on learning.

NASA's resources had also changed. Its civil service headcount had shrunk from a peak of nearly 34,000 at the height of the Apollo program to just under 22,000 by the year of the *Challenger* accident.[9] As the workforce grew smaller, it also grew older, which meant there was a lower likelihood of young graduates importing new ideas from top university labs into the agency.[10] NASA's budget had fallen from more than 4 cents of every federal tax dollar in the mid-1960s to less than a penny per tax dollar two decades later.[11] Employees were expected to do more with less.

NASA was not alone in struggling to improve project performance during this era. A 1988 RAND study of 52 civilian megaprojects (defined as projects ranging in cost from $500 million to over $10 billion in 1984 dollars) reported an average cost growth of 88 percent. The study also found that new technology posed significant challenges: "The incorporation of new technology in a megaproject almost ensures that the project will make more mistakes than money. The use of new technology is the only factor that is associated with bad results in all three dimensions: cost growth, schedule slippage, and performance shortfalls."[12] This finding would not surprise experienced project or system engineers. The introduction of new technology always represents a significant risk, particularly in spaceflight; there are very limited ways to fix the systems on a rocket or a satellite after launch.

After *Challenger* and a subsequent high-profile investigation, NASA commissioned retired Air Force general Samuel C. Phillips, who had managed the Apollo program at NASA's headquarters in Washington, DC, to lead a study group and make recommendations to the NASA administrator. Among other things, his report called for the agency to "strengthen agency-wide leadership in developing and managing people."[13] This created an opportunity for NASA to find new ways of developing the talent of its project management workforce. One of the most powerful tools it ultimately adopted for sharing knowledge and lessons was storytelling.

Why Stories Work

Stories are a natural form of communication that has always helped humankind convey and distribute information. Some scholars argue that humans are hard-wired to learn from each other in this manner. "Narrative arises from the advantages of communication in social species," writes Brian Boyd, who suggests that narrative has always provided useful knowledge to audiences and status to storytellers.[14] Stories have undoubtedly played an important part of our social evolution, and we have subsequently evolved to listen to them closely and with care. On a more practical level, psychologist Jerome Bruner describes story as one of our primary means of understanding the world: "There are two ways of cognitive functioning, two modes of thought, each providing distinctive ways of ordering experience, of constructing reality. . . . A good story and a well formed argument are different natural kinds."[15]

Stories are legitimate means of explanation. They rely on a narrative arc to initiate and sustain interest in the body of the text, and if the arc is strong enough, the story will stick far more powerfully than a well-done PowerPoint presentation or paper. Bruner performed experiments that showed that stories were 22 times more memorable than flat information with the same content.[16] Since stories are so sticky, they can serve as an efficient and effective method for conveying important information to audiences that don't share the technical knowledge or expertise of the storyteller.

Why? Skilled storytellers bring emotion and passion to their delivery. This has a powerful effect that makes a listener attend to it carefully, and in many cases identify with the teller or protagonist. As a result, stories can lower the defenses of listeners and push them beyond binary cost-benefit thinking to consider alternative perspectives. "Narratives are a performance-enhancing drug for empathy," says Jamil Zaki, a psychologist who leads the Stanford Social Neuroscience Laboratory.[17] Beyond that, stories leave room for the listener to make sense of what she is hearing. She can interpret, fill in gaps, and use her imagination to better understand and grasp meanings.

In a project environment, stories offer five major advantages. First, while databases, training, and other tools for sharing lessons require time and significant cost, storytelling is a low-cost method that needs no training. Few people will say, "I can't tell a story, I don't have that skill." Nearly anyone working on a complex project can share stories of challenges, successes, and failures.

Another advantage of stories is that they require and build the muscles of reflective leadership. Although projects value speed, this often comes at the cost of learning. One of the persistent findings of project failure is a lack of commitment and time for learning and reflection. Storytelling is flexible in its time demands; stories of all lengths can be valuable. When storytelling is accepted as part of an organization's culture, this allows reflective leadership to become a goal and an outcome related to increasing knowledge about complex activities within the organization. The reflective leader or practitioner becomes central to a learning organization in a context that demands the ability to develop, retain, and transfer knowledge.

A third attribute of stories is that they facilitate a communal sense of meaning. This concept is vital in an age of rapid change. When there is little change, a community—a family unit, team, or organization—can establish meaning over time. In a volatile and uncertain environment, a story provides a context in which people can find a shared meaning and purpose. A culture of knowledge is built on the meaning ascribed to agreed-on stories. This is both the power and danger of story: regardless of its accuracy, it creates a shorthand for common understanding. Stories simplify reality, which can be useful for reaching broad audiences, but the process of simplification can introduce distortions that ultimately lead to poor decision-making. It should come as no surprise that stories often drive changes in processes, standards, and leadership direction.

A fourth advantage of stories is that they can provide a sense of clarity about what is important. All organizations and projects have an essential purpose. One of the prime challenges to that purpose is the ability to focus. Nonstop emails and meetings create constant pressure and distractions. Stories can serve as reminders to ignore nonessential activities in favor of vital priorities.[18] A compelling story that encapsulates a mission's purpose and goals can help team members cut through the noise and stay on task.

Finally, stories provide a sense of connection through a strong emotional link. They allow people to share their thoughts and feelings. Storytellers who express vulnerability by revealing their emotional stake in a story model the behaviors associated with psychological safety, which in turn can encourage others to share their perspectives without fear of retribution.

Stories in Knowledge Organizations

Many, if not most, project stories fall into one of three categories: successes, failures, or change initiatives that illuminate the political dimensions of work. *Challenger* is an example of a failure story that has been told in many different ways and shared far and wide outside of NASA. Within an organization, a failure story can prompt reflection that ultimately leads to changes in strategy, governance, processes and procedures, or culture.

The challenge of failure stories is that they are not often easy for organizations to accept. The people involved with the failure may feel persecuted, misunderstood, or otherwise unfairly treated. These dynamics certainly existed at NASA in the immediate aftermath of

both the *Challenger* and 2003 *Columbia* accidents. The deaths of the
crew members weighed heavily on everyone associated with the
shuttle program, and it simply took time until people were ready to
see their own stories as opportunities for learning.

Success stories can build organizational confidence and bolster
morale. They can take a variety of archetypal forms: the upstart versus the established giant (David vs. Goliath), persistence in the face
of terrible circumstances (Job), or the merger that leads to a sum
greater than its parts (love story), to name just a few. Stories about
organizational wins are important, but as engineering historian
Henry Petroski warns, "Success can mask latent flaws."[19]

Political stories can include elements of success or failure, but their
underlying value is in helping practitioners understand the dynamics that shape the project-based organization. These can be stories of
bureaucratic entrepreneurs who worked the system effectively, or of
those who subverted the system in service of the mission, values, or a
higher purpose. Dennis McCarthy, project manager of NASA's Cosmic
Background Explorer, once told Ed in a knowledge-sharing event that
"the system is chicken," meaning that large organizational systems
can sometimes be risk-averse to the detriment of project success.[20]

The use of stories is nothing new in preparing knowledge workers
to make decisions based on complex and sometimes contradictory
information. The case study method, first introduced by Harvard
Business School (HBS) nearly a hundred years ago, has been widely
accepted at schools of business and public policy for decades.[21] The
classic HBS-style case study sets a story in motion and then pauses
at a key decision point, providing readers an opportunity to reason,
reflect, and discuss possible approaches. When used in a classroom
setting, the actual outcome of the story is often revealed only after a
facilitated dialogue draws out different perspectives about the challenges facing the protagonists. The professors who pioneered the use
of cases at HBS took inspiration from the casebook tradition in use at
law schools, which in turn relied on the Socratic method to sharpen

legal reasoning among lawyers in training. Legal cases are narrative in nature. When lawyers and judges consider precedent, they set one story next to another and decide if the two are analogous.

Even as graduate schools that train professionals recognized the role that stories could play in educating knowledge workers, it took longer for many knowledge organizations to adopt storytelling as an accepted practice for learning and development. At NASA, storytelling caught on almost by accident, and it took years before many hard-bitten engineers would accept that a "soft" activity could provide real value in a technical organization.

The Introduction of Stories at NASA

One outcome of the *Challenger* era was the establishment of NASA's first-ever initiative to provide professional development for project managers. Ed, whose background as an organizational psychologist made him unlike anyone else at the agency, quickly bumped into the limitations of traditional training. He knew NASA's culture would demand learning from in-house project management experts rather than consultants peddling off-the-shelf lessons. These veterans had the knowledge, but many of the instructors he recruited for the first classes simply presented slides and lectured in a less-than-engaging fashion.

But Ed saw that one senior project manager from Goddard Space Flight Center did things completely differently. Jerry Madden would simply tell stories. No slides, theories, or scripted presentations; instead, he shared actual experiences. And at a time when most NASA project managers still wore ties to work, Madden would leave the tie at home when leading one of these sessions. The success of Madden's approach pointed the way toward knowledge-sharing events that focused on stories rather than traditional training.

A knowledge-sharing event relying on stories begins by rejecting the premise of one-size-fits-all answers: rather than focusing on *the* way to solve a problem, the emphasis on personal story makes it clear there is *a* way to address a particular context. This is a vital advantage. It assumes the validity of many different perspectives, interpretations, and answers. It encourages diversity of opinion and thought.

And at NASA, storytelling elevated the events above training, which many leaders and subject experts would avoid as something foisted on them by human resources. Knowledge-sharing forums were a chance to involve colleagues and tell their side of the story. Training was boring. Stories were captivating.

Knowledge-sharing forums were not an overnight success at NASA. Branding mattered. For starters, there was a fairly strong prejudice against the word *story* itself. The speakers were often very senior engineers who felt that describing a serious talk on the space shuttle as a story would be degrading and insulting to all concerned. For this reason, these sessions were called Masters Forums at the beginning. There was little mention of "story" in the event announcements or descriptions. The term *Masters Forum* indicated that individuals with expertise in projects were coming together to discuss their experiences and lessons. The events were curated to be inclusive, so that practitioners with diverse backgrounds and broad-based project expertise would feel welcome and participate.

Storytellers also varied in abilities. Some speakers were happy to try a new and possibly more effective approach, but the majority were wary of it. Several members of Ed's team were assigned to work with speakers who were initially reluctant to move away from stilted technical presentations toward more conversational reflections on their experiences. Eventually, almost everyone came around to the realization that stories worked well. At the end of the very first Masters Forum, which was held in 2000, several senior NASA executives approached Ed and said, "We are not sure what this session was, but we liked it." The proof of concept arrived in participant evaluations and increasing attendance. It helped that a few highly regarded engineers embraced the use of stories. Word spread about these early champions, creating a sense that it was okay to follow their lead. And as broadband internet became the norm, videos of compelling stories from forums could be shared with the world.

The first forums were not thematic but deliberately open to all kinds of stories. After the *Columbia* failure, events often targeted particular topics aimed at stimulating honest dialogue. This helped practitioners become comfortable sharing stories of failure and mistakes.

Eventually there were knowledge-sharing forums that addressed specific programs or challenges. An ambitious series of events focused on bringing together alumni of the space shuttle program as NASA prepared to close out shuttle operations in 2011. Program executives from the early days provided evergreen insights about the political savvy necessary to manage stakeholders in the White House and Congress. Engineers recounted the reasoning behind decisions that ended up shaping the program's trajectory. Representatives from private industry, academia, and NASA's international partners were invited to share stories of their roles as well.

At the same time that Ed was convening the early Masters Forums, he developed a series of publications that culminated in an award-winning journal called *ASK Magazine*. *ASK* primarily featured first-person stories from NASA practitioners. From the beginning, it set a tone that was conversational rather than technical. Issue 1 featured a story by Michelle Collins that began: "I was a new engineer at one of NASA's contractor sites, straight out of college and ready to conquer the agency. Of the 120 engineers there, I was the only female. To say I stuck out is putting it mildly."[22]

ASK welcomed a wide range of practitioner perspectives, not just war stories from veterans of the good old days. Since many NASA experts were not professional writers, Ed enlisted a team, including Larry, Matt, and Don Cohen (who has written our case study of the International Space Station in chapter 6), to help capture and edit these stories. The magazine eventually expanded to bring in relevant stories from experts outside NASA as well. As word spread about *ASK*, researchers began to cite its stories in other publications. Ed also began a monthly newsletter that enabled more frequent communication than *ASK*, which was published on a quarterly basis.

Storytelling was *not* a cure-all for the performance of NASA's projects, however. Even as the first generation of forums and publications got underway in the mid- to late 1990s, NASA experienced high-profile failures in its Mars program. A report on these failures by the Government Accountability Office in January 2002 found "fundamental weaknesses in the collection and sharing of lessons learned agency-wide."[23] The loss of the space shuttle *Columbia* in February of 2003 also raised pointed questions about what NASA had learned from *Challenger*.

But by the time NASA was reckoning with the aftermath of *Columbia*, some of NASA's new senior leaders and top engineers were the same people who had attended the early storytelling forums. They now championed these activities in real time while addressing significant challenges.

One example of this culture change can be found in the activities preceding the launch of space shuttle *Endeavour* on mission STS-119 to the International Space Station, which was initially scheduled for launch on February 12, 2009. The previous shuttle flight, STS-126, had experienced a malfunction with a flow control valve on ascent during its launch on November 14, 2008. The anomaly did not endanger the flight, but the engineering team on the ground knew that this would require immediate attention after the mission.

Work began as soon as the shuttle landed safely, but efforts to understand the problem and characterize the risk proved elusive. The pressure to solve this quickly was well understood by everyone in the shuttle program: STS-119 needed to complete its work at the International Space Station by March 26 in order not to interfere with a Russian Soyuz mission to the station.

All decisions for complex programs involve a series of tradeoffs based on risks. The decision-making pressure stacking up for STS-119 was similar to that of *Challenger* and *Columbia*. In this case the team responded dramatically differently.

One of the final reviews before any shuttle launch was a Flight Readiness Review, which would convene the space shuttle program managers at Kennedy Space Center along with NASA's engineering and safety communities to review the mission and vote "go" or "no go." When the program made its case to launch on schedule at the Flight Readiness Review in February, the engineering and safety communities voted "no go," saying the program had failed to adequately characterize the risk associated with the flow control valve. It took two more Flight Readiness Reviews until a technical solution emerged that assured the engineering and safety communities that the risk could be managed. NASA was able to launch STS-119 in the nick of time before it would have posed a significant schedule problem at the space station.

Shortly after the mission, NASA chief engineer Mike Ryschke-witsch requested a case study about the contentious decision-making process leading up to the launch of STS-119.[24] This represented a 180-degree shift from just a few years earlier. The story that emerged in that particular case study captured glimmers of the culture shift that had taken place at NASA in the post-*Columbia* era. After one of the difficult "no-go" Flight Readiness Reviews, Joyce Seriale-Grush, the chief engineer of the space shuttle orbiter, told Ryschkewitsch, "This was really hard and I'm disappointed that we didn't have the data today, but it feels so much better than it used to feel."[25] NASA had changed since *Columbia*, and leaders like Ryschkewitcsh were committed to letting the technical community know that it was safe to speak up. He commissioned the case study as a way of socializing what had just happened: dissenting opinions had been met with respect rather than scorn or disregard. The process had worked.

The Growth of Organizational Storytelling

NASA is not the only organization to use stories for these types of purposes. Some organizations have used stories to create common meanings among new employees. Larry worked for years at IBM, and the orientations he would run relied on many stories of its fabled history to bond new employees to the firm. Several of the US intelligence agencies use stories for the same effect. The 9/11 Commission decided to release its findings in a narrative format that more closely resembled a spy thriller than a government report, and it shot up the bestseller list.[26] The National Intelligence Council, an open source think tank within the intelligence community that brings in outside experts, uses narrative-based scenarios to describe the geopolitical trends it foresees. (A scenario it published in 2008 predicted the COVID-19 global pandemic with chilling accuracy.)[27]

One of the most detailed and interesting examples of how stories were introduced to a project-based organization is recounted in *The Springboard* by Stephen Denning.[28] Denning was a country and regional manager at the World Bank when he was tapped to work on knowledge issues. In this role he was frustrated by the excessive dependence on slides and strictly linear models of explanations prevalent at the bank. Almost accidentally, Denning started using stories to make some of his arguments at the many meetings he attended. He eventually came to realize that this was often more effective than his previous presentation style, and he began to use this technique more and convinced members of his team and colleagues to do the same. The presentation culture of the bank was never the same after that.

The boom in storytelling through popular formats such as TED Talks and The Moth has spread to the business world as well. Countless organizations have now hosted TED-like events to give employees an opportunity to share their stories. If nothing else, this trend serves as a clear indication of the growing acceptance of personal stories in professional settings. When it comes to creating meaning and organizing reality, stories are as legitimate a tool as any other, and they have finally reached a wide level of acceptance and appreciation in even seemingly hostile cultures. They will likely never be an underused asset again.

Putting Stories to Work

When asked about the most effective tool for changing the culture of an organization, we recommend stories. There are many ways that teams can bring stories to an organization.

1. Be clear about the goals for using stories. Ed's efforts to promote the use of stories at NASA started with three goals. The first was to create a culture of reflective leadership and practitioners. Project teams often struggle with finding the time necessary for learning and conversation. This is understandable, but it creates a dangerous environment in which team members feel they cannot take time to learn and share ideas, concerns, and solutions. The second goal was to encourage the use, creation, and exchange of stories. At NASA we initially tracked the number of stories shared and their themes. (Eventually social media made it possible to track sharing in a much more granular way.) The third goal was to promote knowledge sharing through conversation.

2. Start every project by telling your story. Every project starts with a story. Projects are always about delivering value through products or services. The journey to arrive at that value is the story. Like projects, stories start with a problem. When you begin a project, ask the question, "What is the story we are hoping to tell on completion?" Note where the discussion goes. Is there agreement on the goals? Are there subplots? What different stories emerge? What are we learning about the project? Do all team members give voice to the story?

3. Make room for presentations as stories. Many organizations train people to provide formal slide presentations that are organized by logical thinking. Create places and spaces for presentations that are structured as stories as well. During knowledge-sharing forums at NASA, we would often ask presenters to tell a brief story about a success or failure without any slides in fifteen minutes or less. The practitioners quickly understood how to spell out the problem, context, approach to problem-solving, and outcome. The attendees would then extrapolate lessons from the story, which often differed from those of the presenter. This process encouraged practitioners to share perspectives rather than sell a viewpoint.

4. Offer storytelling workshops. Although telling stories can be natural and easy for many people, it is also a great skill to develop. Today there are many professionals with expertise in storytelling. At NASA, we arranged a session with Annette Simmons, author of *The Story Factor: Inspiration, Influence, and Persuasion through the Art of Storytelling.*[29] This created an appreciation among project professionals, scientists, and engineers of the value of this practice. Consider a team-learning session by inviting a specialist in stories to help build this capability among your people. There are also plenty of excellent resources about stories by authors ranging from David Hutchens and Nancy Duarte to Stephen King.

5. Stories can be oral, written, or visual. We have focused our discussion mostly on oral stories, but some storytellers are more comfortable expressing their ideas in writing. And at some NASA knowledge forums we hired visual storytellers to illustrate the stories that were shared. The enduring popularity of graphic novels over the past several decades has made it clear that stories with pictures aren't just for kids.

6. Run experiments and iterate. There are many ways to bring story into an organization. If a first attempt doesn't work, try a different approach. The key is to realize that stories are an essential tool to stimulate conversation, encourage reflection and learning, promote diverse voices, and inspire purpose. Some of the best organizations in the world understand this and take the time to build this powerful capability.

4
Culture

Culture eats strategy.

—attributed to Peter Drucker

For several years, Ed reported the status of the NASA project academy to General Jack Dailey, NASA's associate deputy administrator for much of the 1990s. General Dailey had previously served as assistant commandant of the Marine Corps. One day Ed asked him, "What is the difference between executive leadership at NASA and the Corps?" General Dailey said both organizations were led by mission-driven, smart, passionate, and patriotic people, but there was one key difference. While serving in his final role in the Marines, he arrived early one morning at a hangar for a flight on a military aircraft. It was a dismal, wet day, and in an offhand way he said to his aide, "Why are these hangars painted this depressing gray? Why aren't they purple so there's more energy?" He returned to the hangar at the end of the day to find it painted bright purple. His glib observation on a dreary morning had been interpreted as an order. NASA, he said, was completely different: direct orders were seen as nothing more than a reason for dialogue. That's the power of organizational culture.

Culture is one of the most complex words in the English language, and it can be used to describe everything from an individual's love of opera (a cultured person) to something that grows in a petri dish. It is often used as a cop-out in discussions of organizational behaviors that cannot be easily explained. When someone says, "It's the culture," that usually ends a discussion since there is rarely a consensus about what culture is, much less a consensus as to how to change it. An old bit of folklore says that "culture is how employees act when no one is looking."

We are going to define culture for our purposes as the mostly unwritten yet enduring rules of behavior that convey "how things get done around here." Organizational culture acts as a powerful addendum to rule books and other formal sources of behavioral control. Anyone who works at an organization for even a short time begins to pick up on the signals, stories, and artifacts that compose the culture.

Since culture is so elusive and complex, we are going to limit this chapter to the three dimensions of it that are most salient to our overall discussion: collaboration, valuation of knowledge, and trust. There is some overlap among these ideas—we don't mean to suggest that they should be considered stand-alone behaviors—but they are also observable in practice, and they have a very strong effect on the culture of an organization.

No organization wants to be perceived as having an inferior or outdated culture. We have worked with many that claimed to have a "learning" or "collaborative" culture, but on close examination, they were operating under the less fashionable command-and-control model. This model was first developed due to a great leap in technology that made large-scale projects feasible in the mid- to late nineteenth century. The work was usually industrial in nature, such as manufacturing tools, machines, chemicals, clothing, or electrical and transportation equipment. It was more complex than anything undertaken by family businesses in earlier times, and it required a far more sophisticated management and financial structure to function efficiently.

The only model for managing a much larger workforce that performed complex tasks over a range of geographies was the military, which was based on a command-and-control structure that was organized and led by a rigid hierarchy. All the knowledge in such organizations went in one direction—top-down—and with the exception of intelligence, there was little opportunity for knowledge acquired by a worker to ever reach the head office where knowledge was developed, sorted, and distributed on a need-to-know basis through the command structure. Since the military was highly regarded and very familiar in the United States and most of western Europe, the model wasn't too difficult to replicate in organizations sprouting up in these countries. It quickly spread elsewhere as well.

This operating philosophy could be summarized in a quote apocryphally attributed to Henry Ford: "What do I want with a worker's brain? I only want his arm." The idea of optimizing this insight for peak production was codified by Frederick Taylor and labeled "scientific management." Virtually no one discussed workplace culture in those years or for decades to come. Command-and-control culture became ubiquitous, though unions disrupted some of its more repressive and difficult practices such as Taylorism and the scientific management movement. And though workers have always generally despised it, this model still thrives under various names and guises around the world today.

As command-and-control evolved over decades, it helped produce a staggering increase in wealth and human well-being. During the past 150 years, global per capita gross domestic product has increased more than tenfold.[1] But the great limitation of this model was (and is) its reliance on the physical strength of humans and machines as the key source of wealth production. This type of production factor and its associated activities can be far more easily measured, managed, traded, and priced than the major factor of production today, which is knowledge.

While visiting a Google campus in New York City, Ed and Larry
were struck by the energy flowing throughout the site. People were
talking, eating together, and bumping into one another as they settled into temporary workspaces for an hour or a day. The spirit of
knowledge development was something akin to what the Japanese
call *ba*, the positive spirit of a place that you can feel in the air. It was
as far from command-and-control as one can get because it focused
on the development and movement of knowledge rather than the
use of power to control it.

The *ba* that Larry and Ed observed at Google was not the result
of an open floor plan, ping-pong tables, or the availability of kombucha and cold brew on tap 24 hours a day. When Matt sat down
with the head of learning and development at a high-flying venture
capital–backed business, he remarked on the abundance of amenities, friendly dogs, and brightly colored furniture in the company's
headquarters. The executive rolled her eyes and said that appearances
masked a darker reality: psychological safety was lacking throughout
the organization. On the flip side, many NASA facilities date to the
early 1960s, with government-issue furniture and no free coffee, and
NASA is regularly voted the best place to work in the federal government.[2] A well-designed space may enable sociability that enhances
collaboration, but the physical trappings do not make the culture.

We don't mean to suggest that Google is a nonhierarchical paradise, but even at a glance its culture provides an illuminating contrast with the notion of Ford's assembly line a century ago. Google
doesn't care much for the strength of its employees' arms, but it
surely cares about what's in their brains. If anything, Google has historically placed a premium on engineering talent above all else.[3] To
be clear, the prioritization of perceived engineering ability can also
lead to a less-than-ideal working environment for women, people

of color, and others who have historically been underrepresented in predominantly male engineering organizations.

A great benefit of a culture that prizes knowledge is that it serves as a competitive advantage against cultures that are slower to change. One of the most sweeping changes of the past two decades has been the agile movement, which empowers people at the local level to get things done. Whatever tools, processes, and systems an organization has in place, culture ultimately determines the extent to which it streamlines decision-making and facilitates productivity. Economist Joel Mokyr has coined the term *culture of growth* to identify culture as the defining factor that leads to the beliefs, values, and associated behaviors necessary for organizational success, and, ultimately, the creation of societal wealth.[4]

Collaboration

Like the word *culture*, *collaboration* has several definitions, and is often used to mean "cooperation" or "plays well with others." But collaboration implies acts of working together that are voluntary and often directed or prompted by the organizational culture. For example, when a colleague asks for assistance with a difficult problem and you offer to help even if you don't have a way to bill for your time, that's collaboration. It often manifests as a proactive attitude that can be seen in actions such as reading an article and sending it to a colleague in another department who might find it useful. Even if you hardly know the person, you are helping.

Organizational cultures do not develop in a vacuum. Organizations are part of the larger cultures in which they operate, and as such they reflect the values of those places. The United States has both an individualistic and a collegial culture that can be tapped into by an employer to incorporate its own cultural preferences, but it's not always easy to reconcile these two contrasting attitudes. This may help account for the noted difficulties of many change management projects. All three of us have worked with global firms and organizations and have experienced the ways in which, for instance, Japanese culture affects the work culture of Japanese firms, just as American culture influences the norms of American organizations.

Most organizational cultures fall somewhere on a continuum between promoting competition or collaboration. In environments that heavily incentivize individual competition, there is usually little willingness to help colleagues voluntarily, while at the other end of the spectrum there are cultures that are successful at encouraging collaboration for a variety of reasons. Mission-oriented workplaces, for instance, often have collaborative cultures. NASA is a classic example: the agency's mission (space exploration and scientific research) is the prime directive, and people think of it that way and refer to it in everyday conversation as well as in more formal communications. The very phrase "mission-critical," which is used in organizations ranging from the military and intelligence agencies to hospitals, implies extensive collaboration.

But for the many people working in organizations that fall somewhere between dog-eat-dog and fully mission driven, there are plenty of examples of how collaboration can be baked into the culture. A good case study is IBM in the early 1990s. The company was in the doldrums, and it appointed a new CEO from outside the technology industry: Louis Gerstner. Among his earliest actions was to change the way bonuses were allocated. Bonuses had been based predominantly on an individual's achievements for the year. This was something of an industry standard, but it was not always the case in the consulting industry where Gerstner had previously worked. At IBM he changed the formula for allocation to a three-part system consisting of individual accomplishments, division or unit achievements, and overall firm performance.

Larry was an executive at IBM at this time, and he can attest to the uproar this change initially caused. Most of the objections focused on worries about free riding, but it turned out that almost all employees welcomed the idea of shared rewards, and this dramatically shifted behaviors from individualist to collective thinking. This helped launch IBM into a considerable rebound in profits and productivity. It was one of IBM's most effective changes during Gerstner's tenure as CEO. One could say that the sort of collaboration ensuing from this change was based on self-interest, and there is an element of truth to that. But the observable collaboration that occurred eventually became a habit for many employees, and it seeped into the culture.

There are other ways collaboration can be induced in a culture. The CEO of Russell Reynolds, a prestigious executive search firm, once turned down the opportunity to hire a very well-known recruiter who would have brought the firm a considerable amount of revenue. But this potential rainmaker was a solo player, nice but not at all interested in working with others or sharing his very extensive network of leads, clients, and potential candidates. This decision caused controversy in the organization, but it was quickly dispelled by the CEO's argument that the value of the firm's culture was worth far more than the revenue that would be generated by this lone wolf.

In a similar vein, Square, which competes for talent with giants like Google and Apple, safeguards its collaborative culture by walking away from superstars who show up with egos to match their technical skills. "There are people who are damn good and really good with other people, versus prima donnas who are impossible to work with," says senior software engineer Ray Ryan.[5]

Netflix goes so far as to lay out the core principles of its culture on the jobs page of its website, and it emphasizes the extent to which its employees "share information openly, broadly, and deliberately." It also explicitly states that its "core philosophy is *people over process*," and it identifies collaboration as an outcome of the culture this philosophy fosters.[6]

One way organizations tip the scales in this direction is by following what Stanford's Robert Sutton has dubbed "the no asshole rule."[7] Sutton clearly documented the negative effects brought about by hiring and retaining people who do not play well with others. There is no stronger signal that radiates through a firm than perceptions of the personal qualities of the people who get promoted or hired. Choosing people who collaborate well with others is a not-too-subtle way of recognizing the behaviors the company seeks to cultivate in its employees. Companies ranging from Berkshire Hathaway to IDEO have followed this dictum for years, as has Mozilla, a nonprofit that creates open-source software. The open-source software development movement is inherently collaborative, which makes people who engage in toxic behaviors a significant liability to any organization operating in that ecosystem.[8]

Valuing Knowledge

About 30 years ago, a well-known and well-connected consultant we know found about a hundred firms that claimed to be either a "learning organization" or an "organization that values its employees' knowledge above all else." These declarations were often found in the opening paragraphs of annual reports or mission statements. This consultant then called executives in these organizations and asked them what exactly made them a learning or knowledge-valuing firm. The two most common responses he received were: 1) the training budget, and 2) modest bonuses for fewer than 1 percent of employees who'd had some innovative idea. Needless to say, he was not impressed with these answers. Nor are we.

Today, few organizations take concrete steps to demonstrate the value they place on knowledge. How many actually refer to knowledge in employee evaluations or in recruitment listings? We are not talking about R&D units—we mean knowledge found in the day-to-day activities of all employees, regardless of their function. It is this sort of valuation of knowledge that leads to an enduring cultural understanding of its importance.[9]

One of the most effective ways to foster a culture that values knowledge is by creating and elevating knowledge communities within an organization. As we mentioned in chapter 2, the NASA Engineering & Safety Center, created in response to the space shuttle *Columbia* accident, established an elite community of engineers that quickly became a source of expertise for stakeholders and customers seeking knowledge for a variety of challenges. This is an example of promoting a knowledge culture by creating a community of readily available talent. The status of this organization helped to incentivize NASA's technical workforce to adopt positive attitudes toward knowledge, collaboration, and a culture of technical excellence.

The establishment of the NASA project academy years earlier had sent another set of signals about the value the agency placed on knowledge. As the academy had expanded beyond its original focus on training, the publications, forums, and other events it sponsored used storytelling as a strategy to disseminate messages about the culture. For instance, an article that ran in *ASK Magazine* was the first-person story of an engineer named Dustin Gohmert, who designed a new seat for astronauts on the Orion crew capsule in his garage over Christmas vacation.[10] His personal account spoke to ingenuity, resourcefulness, and a love for hands-on work, all qualities that NASA seeks to imbue in its engineers through its culture.

As we mentioned in chapter 1, another way that organizations foster a culture that values knowledge is by funding individual knowledge exploration. Many organizations have budgets for employees to attend conferences or engage in exchanges with peers, professors, and other experts. Bringing in guest speakers or sponsoring visiting fellows also demonstrates a commitment to knowledge while making it available to a wider audience within the organization.

One of the most fun ways we have seen a firm put knowledge front and center was at GLG, an expert network that has built its entire business model around connecting its clients directly with people who have the knowledge they need. In its New York headquarters, the lobby area doubles as a book nook featuring several shelves of eclectic titles. The meeting rooms throughout the space are named after great thinkers and writers from Socrates to Keynes. There is more to culture than trappings, as we said earlier, but these visual cues serve as a constant reminder that ideas are what matter.

Trust

As with the other themes of this chapter, *trust* also has multiple meanings, which leads to ambiguity when it is applied to organizations and human behavior. For our purposes, a key consideration is how a lack of trust can influence knowledge sharing. If colleagues in a large organization don't trust one another, the process of eliciting knowledge from them comes with higher transaction costs. Nothing is harder in a culture with a trust deficit than moving knowledge when there is no mandate to do so.

Some of the most common questions that arise when trust is lacking include: Will I get credit if the person I am helping uses my response in a paper or talk? Will this person reciprocate if I need assistance? Will I be besieged with more queries? Is it worthwhile to help this person because of her place in the hierarchy?

In these and many other ways, trust plays a strong role in enabling, hampering, or even blocking knowledge transfer. Between the value of time and lost opportunities, the costs can be very considerable. So what can be done? One of the most effective tools for building a culture of trust is simply saying, "I trust you to do the right thing." Backing those words with action shows people that you're serious.

Larry once had about 40 people reporting to him in a research unit of a major consulting firm. As a manager, he was expected to read and approve all travel and expense forms. Since many of these consultants traveled extensively, this would have meant spending a half-day or more on paperwork each week. This struck him as a tremendous waste of time and energy that did not add any value to his unit. At a group meeting, he told the team that he trusted them to stay at a Marriott rather than a Four Seasons hotel, and that he wasn't going to dive into their expense reports. He realized that the cost of not trusting the group would be far greater than an infrequent upgrade from coach to business class. This not only gave Larry time to do more worthwhile work, but it added to the group's social capital.[11] They knew they were trusted and proved to be trustworthy over the years.

Netflix adopted a more expansive version of the same idea when it abolished its vacation policy and told employees it trusted them to manage their own approach to vacation time. This was an extension of one of its core principles: "Avoid rules."[12] Although the company underwent a learning curve as it put this into practice, it stuck to the essential premise that its knowledge workers should be trusted to get the job done rather than being bound by one-size-fits-all policies.[13] Good behavior is as contagious as bad behavior, and often the best one can do in many situations is to "brighten the corner where you are"—act trustworthy and assume trustworthy behavior from others.

One of the fastest ways to establish trust is with face-to-face meetings. There is a body of research that finds that when people have met face to face, maybe even just a few times, they are able to establish swift trust. This alone is a solid argument for occasionally bringing together employees of geographically dispersed organizations. There is also evidence that cross-organization communication increases after face-to-face meetings, as does the development of new ideas.[14] In the wake of the pandemic, organizations will strive to find ways to balance the benefits of face-to-face meetings with the efficiencies and conveniences of virtual work.

Like collaboration, trust tends to be more of a given in mission-critical organizations. The mission serves as such a strong force that trust is automatically presumed critical to the success of the mission. When Ed and Larry asked a group of cancer researchers about the issue of trust, they looked puzzled by the very question. One of them replied, "Of course we trust one another—not only within our firm but with our peers throughout the world. We are fighting cancer!"

Culture Change

As we have said, organizational culture is largely associated with longstanding norms and behaviors that define how things get done, and it is shaped by broader forces in society. What if, in an era of remote and virtual work on globally dispersed teams, this concept no longer holds true?

Ask most people what makes organizational change difficult, and they will mention culture. The durability of beliefs and values helps explain why change initiatives often meet resistance and inertia. This durability is a sign of a strong culture, which has traditionally been considered a positive attribute of successful firms.

At the very beginning of Ed's NASA career, he had a mentor who told him that he would have a great future at the agency if he slowed down. "You don't understand how NASA works, but over time you will learn what you need to know. You need to talk less and listen more, and eventually it will all make sense," he said. When Ed asked how long this process might last, his mentor replied that it would take about ten years. Ed laughed to himself at the idea of holding his tongue for a decade.

This story illustrates an important but not obvious point: strength without flexibility turns culture into a straitjacket that constricts growth and access to a wide range of knowledge and ideas. In an era when organizations increasingly recognize the value of diverse, agile teams exercising authority at the local level, the idea of culture as a monolithic thing shared by an entire organization may be on its way out. One thing is for certain: just as organizational culture today no longer resembles the era when all IBM men were expected to dress identically in dark suits and wingtip shoes, the future will likely see a further devolution of the notion of a centralized culture.[15]

Culture Change at NASA after *Challenger* and *Columbia*

The 1986 *Challenger* accident devastated NASA. It led to major reviews and efforts to improve the agency, including Ed's assignment to work on establishing the Program/Project Management Initiative, the precursor to NASA's current-day project academy.[16] But despite new initiatives to train its younger generation in the aftermath of *Challenger*, NASA culture did not change significantly between that accident and *Columbia*. Those young employees were not yet in positions of power, and the older leaders who could have made a difference saw *Challenger* as an aberration within what they viewed as an otherwise successful culture.

It wasn't until a decade after *Challenger* that Columbia University sociologist Diane Vaughan coined the term *normalization of deviance* to describe the role that NASA's culture had played in the accident: "In the years preceding the *Challenger* launch, engineers and managers together developed a definition of the situation that allowed them to carry on as if nothing was wrong when they continually faced evidence that something was wrong."[17] The normalization of deviance had remained a problem within NASA, as the board that investigated the *Columbia* accident noted in its report.[18]

NASA only truly began to change after the *Columbia* accident. A new administrator, Michael Griffin, started by calling for the establishment of a new, vastly simplified governance model that placed greater emphasis on organizational values and shared decision-making power across the organization. This coincided with the rise of a generation of leaders who were early in their careers at the time of *Challenger* and ready to leverage their education and experiences. There was widespread recognition of the dangers of bureaucracy, and an emphasis on communicating with greater transparency and creating a culture in which dissenting opinions were not just tolerated but welcomed. (See the anecdote in chapter 3 about the decision-making process leading up to the launch of space shuttle flight STS-119.)

Organizational cultures will always change more quickly in response to massive shocks such as a tragic accident or a global pandemic than to well-intended, well-planned initiatives. Even so, a dysfunctional culture is not always doomed. With committed leadership and a clear set of guiding principles, organizations can become more collaborative and trusting, which is a prerequisite for success whenever knowledge is the primary factor of production.

Putting Culture to Work

Since culture is mostly defined by collective behaviors and beliefs, it is a difficult intangible to change effectively. With that caveat in mind, here are some mechanisms that we have seen work in organizations that have deliberately shifted their cultures.

1. Signals and messages. Some of the strongest messages that managers and leaders send out are through hiring and promotion. These actions tell employees a story about the beliefs and behaviors that the organization values. This is particularly important when trying to build a collaborative culture: it is impossible to do so while promoting noncollaborative people.

2. Social infrastructure. The way an organization uses and allocates physical space speaks to its attitudes about who matters and how work gets done. Spaces can be designed to encourage conversations and serendipitous encounters by providing simple signals for social interactions, such as coffee and snacks.

3. Valuing learning and ideas. By subsidizing subscriptions to publications, encouraging conference attendance, and developing knowledge networks, an organization demonstrates its commitment to acquiring new knowledge and ideas. Much like hiring and promotion, the ways that an organization recognizes and shares new ideas also lets employees know what really matters.

4. Shared mission and purpose. Through stories, examples, and cases, organizations can define their mission and create a sense of common purpose necessary for mission success. This is an important step in becoming a smart organization: a common understanding of the mission eliminates a great deal of noise, conflict, and transaction costs.

5. Eliminate mechanist metaphors for the organization. The image of the organization as a machine of ever-increasing efficiency needs to be eliminated to foster a culture that prizes learning and knowledge. A more human and organic metaphor should replace it, such as the organization as a living entity that feeds on ideas and a passion for the mission, and that reaches outside itself for sustenance as well as relying on internal sources of energy.

5
Teaming

You can't pile together enough good people to make
a great one.

—attributed to Bob Taylor, in *Organizing Genius*
by Warren Bennis and Patricia Biederman

NASA's Solar Terrestrial Relations Observatory (STEREO) mission made history by capturing the first three-dimensional images of the sun and its inner heliosphere. Launched in 2006 from Cape Canaveral, its twin observatories have yielded data that have greatly increased our understanding of the sun and space weather. The mission, a collaboration between NASA and the Johns Hopkins Applied Physics Laboratory (APL), included partners from industry, academia, and international space agencies. The team that designed, developed, and delivered the observatories has been justly recognized for the mission's exceptional performance.

Yet just a few years before launch, the STEREO project was in real trouble and headed for cancellation rather than acclaim. What happened, and how did the team pivot so that the mission was a success? How do some teams work through periods of failure and ultimately attain high performance? In an organization with many project teams, why do some thrive while others struggle?

One of the common mistakes of organizational life is the tendency to believe in the importance of individual development and organizational governance while assuming that smart individuals will figure out how to work effectively with each other once they're thrown together on a project. But understanding what makes a team great is more complicated than that.

Putting Team Performance into Context

Think about the greatest team that you have been a part of. Why do you think of it that way?

"Great" implies several factors. First and foremost, we associate great teams with successful outcomes and results. The 1969 New York Mets were great because they won the World Series. The team behind the Manhattan Project has been judged as great based on the results it achieved. A successful outcome is a prerequisite for greatness.

Although outcomes are essential, there are other factors that matter as well. A compelling mission and purpose influence perceptions of a team's accomplishments. Greg Oldham and Richard Hackman's five-factor model of individual job satisfaction emphasizes the importance of task significance.[1] An analogous characteristic for a team is the notion of compelling work. A project that poses a significant challenge and has a purpose that transcends mere self-interest can contribute to perceptions of greatness. MIT's Human Dynamics Laboratory identifies great teams as those characterized by and "blessed with energy, creativity, and shared commitment to far surpass other teams."[2]

Context also matters. Great teams perform under great pressure. Project teams today work in an inherently complex environment.

Customers demand speed, agility, and ease of use. New technologies and digital capabilities fuel expectations for accelerated team performance and ever-improving customer experiences. A great team is expected to adapt, change, and innovate so that it can continue to perform at its peak tomorrow as well as today.

In the twentieth century, theories of team performance approached the question from a systems perspective featuring inputs, process, and outputs. The input-process-output (IPO) model of teams describes performance over time as well as the factors that influence inputs and outcomes. In 1965, psychologist Bruce Tuckman originally proposed that teams solve problems and achieve success by navigating preordained phases of group development.[3] The model did not attempt to predict team performance, instead providing a frame for anticipating group growth and development through the completion of phases. The popular Tuckman group phase theory depicts a team forming, establishing norms ("norming"), going through a period of conflict ("storming"), performing, and adjourning. In retrospect it is remarkable that such a simplistic model gained enough traction to become nearly universal in its appeal. It offered no insights about performance, but it was a catchy tune that seemed to explain something intuitive about the natural ebb and flow of teams. It also provided a framework for the deliberate consideration of factors that could be designed and improved over time for the goal of high-performance teams.

In a time of little or slow change, it's possible that many teams might go through similar phases in a predictable sequence. But in a period characterized by unending technological disruption, global supply chains, and uncertainty stemming from factors ranging from geopolitics to climate change, phase models don't cut it.

In a world driven by speed, cost sensitivity, flexibility, and results-oriented outcomes, there was a need for a faster model. In the 1990s, the seeds of what would become the agile revolution began to spread in the software and information technology fields. The notion of projects moving through orderly phases according to a waterfall model was disrupted by a movement that placed trust in people to work collaboratively in self-driven teams with minimal documentation, an emphasis on customer-centricity, and a commitment to speed and iterative experimentation. The agile revolution shifted the lens from the IPO systems view to one focused on definable, measurable outcomes.

These two schools of thought about team performance are not exclusive or necessarily competitive. The case can be made that the best teams incorporate lessons from both perspectives. The agile school points to the importance of achieving outcomes and trusting people for collaboration and fast performance. The social science view extends the timeframe to account for the creation of long-duration team capability and maturity. Organizations are under tremendous pressure to be able to deliver fast outcomes and develop mature teams that work well over time.

Thanks in part to the agile movement, team phase and stage models have been supplemented by an understanding of teams as dynamic entities that need to respond and adapt to changing circumstances.[4] The dynamic capabilities framework first identified by David Teece, Gary Pisano, and Amy Shuen in the mid-1990s raises the importance of firms sustaining long-term performance through team-learning routines that support managerial strategy.[5] From this vantage point, teams serve as the bridge between strategy and project outcomes. This framework promotes the importance of teams as the essential drivers of value delivery and strategic innovation in environments characterized by volatility and rapid change. Current research into the importance of individual-, team-, and organization-level performance aligns with our belief that a project's work is affected by whether it is controlled locally at the micro level, by larger organizational factors at the macro level, or at a global level in order to address a complex societal challenge that demands significant political and cultural collaboration.[6]

Another aspect of team performance that is simpatico with the dynamic capabilities framework is the development of sense-and-respond behaviors. As described by Jeff Gothelf and Josh Seiden, this is a vital capability that requires organizations and leaders to take in and interpret data from the environment in ways that allow for quick responses and experimentation.[7] A core aspect of agile work and related methodologies is scanning the environment and using incoming insights to enable rapid adaptations to changing conditions. This can't take place on the same time horizon as a strategic planning process; it must happen at the team level. It requires strong situational awareness and the ability to spot opportunities and mobilize teams to capitalize on them.[8]

Team Failure

A reality of modern work is that complexity, uncertainty, and constant disruption (see chapter 1 for more consideration of dynamic knowledge) increase risks and the likelihood of failures. All complex projects, programs, and product teams face failure. When it inevitably occurs, a team either learns and adopts behaviors that lead to successful performance or it continues to pursue behaviors that promote failure.

Failures in complex projects can be categorized based on their degree of impact. At the earliest and simplest level are mistakes. These occur frequently and have small impacts on the project. Next are mishaps, which represent more significant losses to the project in terms of cost, time, or performance. A mishap is not an ultimate failure, but it is an inflection point for understanding and overcoming or recovering. Finally, there are failures at the project, program, product, or mission level.

As the term suggests, a *mission failure* is catastrophic, leading to a total loss for the organization as well as the team. It calls for a thorough reexamination of the double-loop learning questions mentioned in our chapter 2 discussion of team learning—Were we doing the right things?—as well as the need for a new strategy or a different path. Mission failures often follow earlier mistakes or mishaps that were not adequately addressed. The normalization of deviance that led to the *Challenger* and *Columbia* accidents resulted from mistakes being ignored or rationalized over and over again. When mistakes lead to conversations that seek to understand what happened and respond appropriately, that's a sign of a smart, mature team.

Organizational Barriers to Improving Teams

In order to improve teams, it is necessary to view them with clear eyes. This is problematic because most organizations and leaders like to hide the actual challenges and occasional ugliness of collaboration. The sanitized version of events promotes a vision of success as an orderly process and failure as resulting from inherent flaws. This impedes our understanding of how teams perform and how we can learn to create the conditions for success. A key factor in inconsistent project performance is a reluctance within organizations to look at projects from the standpoint of how people work together.

Project performance happens at the team level. Team members are closest to the work methods, domain expertise, and needs of their customers. Under the right circumstances, they can ignore organizational leadership, which is often too cautious, detached, or slow to respond. The popularity of the agile movement has been a repudiation of bureaucratic management that has helped to reset the balance of power in favor of teams. The strength of organizations like NASA typically resides in giving project units enough autonomy to self-organize and adapt to changing conditions without significant interference from senior leadership.

Team dynamics are vital in knowledge-intensive cultures, as the flow of knowledge is affected by social factors. Teams discover, create, reframe, use, and share knowledge in ways that can either support or limit growth and innovation. They also seek out and evaluate new ways of working, ultimately deciding what to integrate into their routines and practices.

STEREO: Team Distress to Team Excellence

Returning to the case of STEREO, recognition of the importance of team dynamics came from three directions. The first was a phone call from a NASA senior leader directing Ed to provide support for the team because STEREO was failing due to a toxic and dysfunctional culture. That was highly unusual; most requests originated with project teams. Second, NASA had made an organizational commitment to developing the performance of its project teams and their leaders. The importance of this shouldn't be underestimated. Many organizations ignore warning signs of team failure until it is too late to do anything about it. The third was a culture of knowledge sharing and learning developed at NASA's Goddard Space Flight Center (GSFC), home of the STEREO mission.[9]

STEREO was one of the early NASA teams to go through what is called four-dimensional (4-D) leadership, a comprehensive process developed by Charlie Pellerin, a highly regarded astrophysicist who has spent the second half of his career understanding the dynamics of leadership and team performance. The 4-D method supports projects by employing a short survey to collect data about perceptions of the team. In the case of STEREO, the initial data were some of the worst that had been seen at that point.[10]

STEREO's two key players, GSFC and its prime contractor, the Johns Hopkins University APL, had significant cultural differences that bloomed into deep distrust and outright hostility. Both sides cited culture as a problem, which manifested in sharp differences over perceptions of performance, cost, and schedule. These differences led to fights about oversight controls and responsibilities. A project manager described the challenge as an attempt to overcome the culture shock of a shotgun marriage.

During the start of a three-day workshop, the data were presented to team members. For a quiet minute, nobody said a word. Then two of the senior leaders from GSFC and APL indicated the data were accurate, and an embarrassment to the project, NASA, and all the partners involved. This led to rapid, shared acceptance of the problems plaguing the project, and to a verbal commitment to adopt collaborative behaviors that would deliver high performances.

So how did STEREO go from problem child to model project? The first step was taking the time to collect data. Many troubled teams put their heads down and plod through, maintaining the behaviors that created trouble in the first place. Next, the STEREO team leaders and members set aside three days to reflect, understand, communicate, and find a new way to work together. Then they accepted the truth of the survey data. This was a brave step. Confronted with poor performance, many teams either fail to admit reality or become defensive.

STEREO's leadership subsequently participated in multiple team workshops, individual coaching sessions, and periodic team reassessments. They developed the ability to practice appreciation, commit to shared goals, and create and adopt positive storylines about the project. Rather than perpetuating narratives that blamed their partners, team members consciously made an effort to tell themselves different stories based on a new shared understanding of the project. They designed an operating agreement that established a "badge-less culture" between the two organizations that would diminish differences between GSFC and APL employees and focus on accountability and commitment to sustained trust. In short, they decided to become a team that valued respect, inclusion, learning, and the open exchange of knowledge.

Teams facing pressure to improve must address the specific behaviors that are driving performance. The STEREO challenge was not unusual. Aerospace research projects are typically international partnerships that cut across industry, government, and academia. These global teaming arrangements force people with strong discipline expertise (and egos) to figure out how to collaborate in settings in which simplistic top-down models of authority won't cut it. This is the norm for projects in our age. The challenge it raises is how to create a team culture that both respects and transcends organizational and cultural differences. A powerful starting point is to encourage behaviors and conversations of appreciation and gratitude for the project. A simple question like "What are you most grateful for as we start working together on this project?" can help build a sense of team unity.

Along these lines, it is essential for teams to discuss their commitment to the shared goal for the project. While this might seem obvious, in reality there is often confusion and disagreement about the specifics of work goals. It is important to allocate time to discuss the mission, purpose, and goals of a project. A team of smart, highly diverse individuals will arrive at different conclusions that can corrode their ability to collaborate if time is not taken to arrive at an understanding of shared goals. Some project leaders use reviews and meetings to ask, "What are the three most important outcomes of the project?" This kind of discussion leads to a stronger team that is clear on its destination and less likely to waste time on distractions.

High-performing teams also expertly use stories and create storylines that promote team commitment, communication, and confidence. As a quick tool for predicting and understanding team performance, listen to the stories that project team members share. Simply ask how a project is going. Projects in distress will often produce stories of frustration, anger, blame, problems, and even illness: "I need to get out of here before this job kills me." Projects in challenging but healthy situations will tell very different stories. They will discuss challenges, obstacles, problems within a context of anticipated success, and trust in the team to pull together through difficult times.

Successful teams are open to data that tell the truth, no matter how ugly. They have direct conversations, hold themselves accountable, and commit to finding a path that works.

Six Conditions that Promote High Performance

We are often asked to describe what a great team looks like. In our experience, great teams are heard more easily than they're seen. They have a sound. They are often noisy. Team members talk, laugh, argue, move, disagree, fight, and celebrate. They create space for each member of the team to speak freely. There is no fear of being too honest. They don't confuse emotional intelligence with politeness; they are not afraid to speak truth to each other even if it might mean hurt feelings as part of the growth process. The best teams also have an emotional connection to their work. There is a shared sense of appreciation and gratitude that can only come from a workplace that values each member of the team. Teams are noisy when people feel comfortable being themselves.

We have watched teams that are hard-working and cautious. They participate and engage, but they overly script conversations with senior leaders and key stakeholders to avoid being called out for mistakes. The quiet and polite appearance of collaboration masks an underlying fear of being wrong. Team members strain their necks to see the reactions of senior leaders. As a result, the team learns little to nothing from these conversations because they're playing a sophisticated game of impression management rather than engaging in an open dialogue.

The sound of success is noisier, energized, combative, and honest. An effective project review is probing, zeroing in on problems and gaps rather than strengths. (A NASA project manager whose father was a baker referred to this as focusing on the hole rather than the donut.) This is uncomfortable, but the best teams set high standards for their performance. They can be ruthless with each other in feedback, but the intent is to ensure the best ideas flow.

While every team is unique, there are actions and behaviors that can promote high team performance: *prioritize the mission, nourish the team, build social capital, maintain meaning and purpose, cultivate resilience*, and *embrace distributed teaming*.

Prioritize the mission. Terry Little, an Air Force program manager who rose to serve as executive director of the Missile Defense Agency, was once assigned responsibility for the Joint-Air-to-Surface (JATS) standoff missile program. When Little arrived, the program was in deep trouble despite the fact that team members were putting in twelve hours a day or longer. After his first day on the job, he realized that nobody he had spoken with had mentioned the project's goals.

The next day he called an all-hands meeting and projected a single slide: "JATS GOAL—AWARD CONTRACTS BY JULY." The goal was simple: to award the government's contracts for the program quickly. In this case, "quickly" meant two months earlier than the previously established target that nobody had mentioned to Little on his first day on the job. The purpose of this goal was to ensure that every member of the team knew exactly where to focus their energies. He told everyone to print out the slide and put it on the walls of their cubicles. Any activity that did not directly involve working toward the goal was to cease.

Nobody talked to Little for the rest of the day, but he saw team members posting printouts of the slide in their cubicles. A few days later, people began coming to him with ideas about how to meet the goal. The result of this risky move was that the team ended up awarding all contracts in June, a month earlier than Little's ambitious goal and three months earlier than initially promised.[11]

The need for focused attention speaks to the challenge of making sense of work in organizations. Karl Weick coined the concept of *sensemaking* to describe the importance people place on making sense of the actions, goals, and behaviors desired in an organization.[12] People waste time on the wrong things and become frustrated when they are unclear about desired outcomes. That frustration breeds skepticism, which contributes to a loss of productivity. Strategies to enhance sensemaking increase understanding and transparency and promote faster and more effective action.

The best teams are clear about their outcome. They know what to prioritize and how to spend their time. "A successful team picks out the 10 to 20 important things of the hundreds they could be doing," says Ray Ryan of Square. "They know what's crucial to fix and what's nice to fix. They understand the difference between a flaw that's embarrassing and one that's fatal when working to make something shippable asap."[13]

The importance of communicating the problem or challenge for a team cannot be overstated. Project team members are goal oriented. Achievement is measured by the outcome. Early in Ed's career, he was consulting internally with the International Space Station program. There was tremendous pressure on the team due to a confluence of political, social, technical, and cost challenges. At one meeting, the program lead and systems engineering lead started shouting and challenging each other to a fight. People looked to Ed as the facilitator to refocus the meeting. He instinctively reached for humor. "Clear the room so we can get this fight over with and get back to work," he said. That got a laugh and broke the tension. The tone of the room immediately changed. It reminded the team what was truly important: the mission.

This works with agile teams as well as long-duration programs. A simple, powerful technique is to periodically ask the team to define and describe the outcome it is working to achieve. This is a natural reflection point that facilitates alignment, and it provides an opportunity for a team to stop and assess whether they are proceeding in the right direction or if there is a need to make changes. Researcher Connie Gersick has found that teams go through extended periods of stasis that are then interrupted by sudden change. Her punctuated equilibrium model indicates that teams start in one direction toward an intended outcome, and then the need for change becomes desirable and welcome at a certain point. The key is to remain clear about the destination.[14]

Nourish the team. High-performing teams nourish their members. We have chosen the word *nourish* deliberately to describe behaviors that enable members of a team to feel a sense of respect, inclusion, and belonging. The dictionary says that to nourish is to promote growth and health.[15] So how do high-performing teams nourish their people?

In 2012, Google began crunching internal data to explain why some of its teams were more successful than others. Project Aristotle aimed to understand the factors associated with the best teams.[16] One important finding of this effort was that the best teams have different leadership approaches, styles, and decision-making methods than other teams. Two factors stood out. On good teams, members spoke in relatively equal proportions—no one dominated conversations—and there was social sensitivity to team emotion. Team members actively participated and ensured a welcoming environment for conversations.

A few years later, a *New York Times* article written and based on research by Anita Woolley, Thomas Malone, and Christopher Chabris created a stir when it asserted that the presence of women on a team promoted "smarter teams."[17] It pointed to increased collective intelligence associated with the ability to judge the mental states of others, or what is known as "theory of mind." On effective teams, members are better at reading emotional cues. Simply having a large proportion of women on a team makes a difference. There is evidence that even in online situations, the same effect is strong. So what explains all this?

While many organizations have traditionally tried to ignore or avoid emotions associated with problems, feelings, and interpersonal dynamics, successful teams have behavioral signatures that encourage and support empathy and open expression of emotion. This may partly explain the finding that the presence of more women on a team promotes higher performance. Women score higher than men on tests of social sensitivity, and this may help make diverse teams more effective at managing emotions.[18]

Psychological safety and the freedom of expression, including dissenting opinions, have a massive impact on team performance. Still, knowing this is one thing and acting on it is another. Humans are pack animals that are strongly influenced by group dynamics and social pressure. In many settings, standing out and being different comes at a high cost. But the fear of speaking up, or of being silenced, also imposes tremendous consequences on organizations. We wrote in chapter 3 about the impact of organizational silence at NASA. The space shuttle *Challenger* and *Columbia* disasters were the most vivid and tragic examples of this. In both cases there was a dysfunctional tendency to inhibit or limit communication. NASA has smart people, many good leaders, and lots of high-performing teams. But unless there is a constant commitment to psychological safety as a norm, any team can lapse into a culture of silence.

This can be particularly challenging with long-running projects that span decades and outlast generations of sponsors and stakeholders. "For the long ones, there's a culture that builds up within the project that's beyond the institution or the larger organizational culture," says Greg Robinson, director of the James Webb Space Telescope program for NASA's Science Mission Directorate. He notes that these projects often communicate a message of exclusion to outsiders: "Leave us alone. We got this."[19]

How does a team instill a commitment to psychological safety? The JPL VITAL project faced a unique challenge in coming together just as the COVID-19 pandemic forced the team to work remotely.[20] "Early on, we didn't actually know each other, and many of us still haven't met each other in person," says Stacey Boland, operations team lead, six months after the project has ended. Even so, the team explicitly worked to foster psychological safety from the start: "People were encouraged to speak up and talk through problems versus only presenting finished products." Video conference technology also helped team members build rapport quickly. "On this project we always had our cameras on during meetings, which is not always the case on other projects," says Carey Weisberg, executive assistant to the VITAL team leaders. "I think this gave our meetings an immediacy and personal feel that was important to keep everyone motivated." Psychological safety is an indicator of a team's health. Its presence signals a strong immune system response to the problems that can stem from silence, exclusion, and intimidation.

Nourishing a team goes beyond psychological safety. Teams that are diverse, inclusive, and respectful are associated with superior performance. We mentioned earlier that great teams are often noisy. Part of the reason for this is that team members challenge each other with opposing views and alternative perspectives. Problems involving complex systems require teams with a wide range of cognitive tools. That means those teams need members who think differently than each other. Scott Page of the University of Michigan coined the term *diversity bonus* to describe the value that a member with new cognitive tools can bring to a team: "If the field or the challenge is complex, then diversity bonuses can exist because different people master different relevant tools."[21]

The Netflix Challenge provides a telling example of the power of diverse teams. In 2006, Netflix announced a public contest to improve the performance of its film recommendation engine. Any team that could achieve a 10 percent improvement in performance would win $1 million. With real money at stake, teams with significant engineering expertise came together to tackle this problem. A year into the contest, a company called BellKor led all others, but it could achieve only an 8.4 percent improvement over the existing technology. It merged first with one rival team and then another notably weaker team that brought complementary strengths to its efforts. Some of the required knowledge was technical and some of it was social, such as understanding the mental models people use to think about and categorize movies when rating them. As Page notes, "In the end, being smart was not enough. That was the key lesson. Exceeding the 10% threshold required different ways of thinking, seeing, solving, and coding."[22]

Some degree of cognitive diversity is a given on interdisciplinary teams; an electrical engineer and a computer scientist will approach the same problem from distinct perspectives. But even on teams where everyone is a software developer, for instance, cognitive diversity can come from team members who enter the profession from different paths. Square's Ryan has found talented developers among both high school graduates and former lawyers: "We're not particularly hung up on where you went to school or if you went to school."[23]

Identity diversity is also critical to staffing project teams with people who think differently than each other. "People from different identity groups will bring different knowledge, experiences, and mental models to the table for consideration, allowing for increased cognitive diversity and therefore better outcomes (predictions, creativity, decision making, problem solving, and so on)," writes Katherine Phillips of Columbia University. "Just like one's functional training in engineering, psychology, or cultural anthropology shapes one's cognitive identity, so too does one's gender, race, cultural background, (dis)ability, and so forth."[24]

Build social capital. In the early years of the NASA project academy, there was a near-total focus on individual competence development through training classes. One of the most popular presenters was Jerry Madden, a highly experienced project manager from NASA's Goddard Space Flight Center who simply sat down and told stories. Most of Madden's best stories were about people. For example, when working on a satellite mission with a partner organization in Germany, his team was often feted with wonderful meals. In appreciation of this, his team decided to return the favor on one of their trips to Germany. They packed their luggage with Texas barbecue sauce and threw a party for their hosts that was a tremendous success. A short time after, a technical issue came up with a broken electrical harness. It was a minor problem, but the expected delay posed a serious schedule challenge. A technician who heard the scheduling conversation asked, "Aren't they the barbecue people?" When he learned it was the same team that had hosted the dinner, he offered to fix the harness during an upcoming lunch break. Madden drew a lesson from that episode: "That's what you need to know about project management: you need a little barbecue sauce."[25]

The story is fun, and it makes people smile. Humans have understood for centuries the importance of breaking bread and sitting down for a drink, which can serve as lubricant for important discussions and deals. It creates a social connection that makes it easier to share opinions and read the reactions of others. This example also reinforces the point we made earlier about nourishing a team so that its members can argue and dissent from a place of psychological safety and mutual respect. Savvy teams draw on cultural ingredients to address problems, adapt, and learn.

Maintain meaning and purpose. When the VITAL project began its sprint to design a new ventilator that could be rapidly assembled using commercial, off-the-shelf parts, Weisberg read this project purpose statement at the beginning of the daily team meeting that she moderated: "To meet the COVID-19 ventilator demand by following a path that is closely aligned with patient needs, medical best practices, production capability, and federal regulations, we will Coordinate for Efficient & Rapid Execution (CERE) of each path so that JPL can design, test, and license a ventilator for integration into hospitals for patient care."[26]

Why does a project team come together to do anything? When a project instills team members with a clarity of purpose, motivation ceases to be a concern; it is intrinsic. Purpose provides fuel that can sustain a team through the inevitable setbacks and conflicts it will encounter. A simple act like reading a purpose statement at the beginning of each team meeting reminds the team why its work matters.

Purpose motivates, but it can only take a team so far. The challenges that a team faces will cause it to struggle, which in turn will transform it on a deeper level. "Struggle creates meaning," says Peter Temes, founder and president of the Institute for Innovation in Large Organizations, "and shared struggle creates shared meaning."[27] The distinction between purpose and meaning may seem like a matter of semantics, but it is worth defining. The *shared purpose* of a team gives it something to keep striving to achieve. The *shared meaning* illuminates the significance of the team's experience to its members. A team can often only identify the shared meaning of a project through after-the-fact reflection and dialogue, particularly on fast-paced projects like VITAL.

Purpose statements and project charters may sound like feel-good exercises, but they are commitments that bind teams together and frame the way they approach their work. In July 2013, Italian astronaut Luca Parmitano was involved in a spacewalk on the International Space Station that nearly turned deadly. His spacesuit helmet suffered a malfunction that caused water to begin filling it. The crew acted quickly and pulled Parmitano back into the Space Station. It appeared that the water buildup was the result of a clogged filter.[28]

The next morning, a furious senior leader at NASA entered Ed's office. "How do you teach these people?" he asked, exasperated. "With all of the resources spent on training, leadership development, communications, and policy, how is this possible?" Ed had not yet heard about the incident and had no idea what had sparked this tirade. He soon found out that the same problem had occurred less than two weeks earlier with the same astronaut, on a similar mission. The space station crew had conferred and deliberately decided not to report the problem. This was stunning. The first rule of operating in a highly dangerous environment like space is that deviations from the norm must be reported immediately and clearly.

The bottom-line explanation was that the crew was certain that the cause of the leak was due to the common problem of a leaky drink bag. They were so certain that they decided not to report the problem and to proceed with their regular activities. Again, when long-running projects create a culture that transcends an organization, the message to outsiders is often "Nothing to see here. We got this." This is a reality for high-performing teams of smart people. They like to be left alone to work and produce exceptional outcomes. Anything that gets in the way of their purpose is seen as a distraction and waste of valuable time. They trust in their own abilities to solve problems, which can lead them to resist anything that makes them stop work and spend time learning and sharing.

The senior executive in Ed's office kept asking how the crew could make such a stupid decision. What was wrong with all the learning and development from Ed's team?

Ed responded with a question: "Within the project charter, is there any mention of the requirement for a sustained practice of learning, sharing knowledge, training, and reflection?"

There was a long silence. "No."

A strong sense of purpose can be a double-edged sword. Some teams like to brag about their speed and agility. A team unbound by rules can make decisions faster and outperform teams constrained by too much oversight. But every situation is different. There are decisions that involve low to minimal risk. A failed decision in such instances can be painlessly repaired, but there are other situations where a faulty decision can cause severe damage and even loss of life.

Decisions require an understanding of context, and mission purpose requires striking a balance between getting the job done and building in time for dialogue and learning. The best teams consider the variables and commit to a purpose that accounts for outcomes, people, and reflection.

Cultivate resilience. As we wrote earlier, the space shuttle *Challenger* accident in January 1986 had a profound impact on NASA. The entire agency shared the emotional shock and pain over the loss of the crew. The accident also threw NASA into chaos. Missions that had been designed and scheduled for launch on a space shuttle had to find new ways to get to space while the shuttle program was grounded.

One mission that was affected was the Cosmic Background Explorer (COBE), a science project searching for types of radiation that many physicists, including COBE project scientist John Mather, thought might be artifacts of the big bang. The day after the *Challenger* accident, COBE project manager Dennis McCarthy convened the project team to find a way forward. The team spent the next several months exploring all the possible launch vehicle options in the world. At one point, McCarthy got in hot water with NASA headquarters for reaching out to the French aerospace company Ariane outside the chain of command to discuss the prospect of launching COBE on one of their rockets. As far as he was concerned, his "job was to get this thing into space, whatever the way." The eventual solution, which McCarthy sketched on the back of a napkin, required a radical redesign of the COBE spacecraft. He reconfigured the team's workspace into a so-called skunkworks bullpen (a nickname associated with a legendary Lockheed aircraft development team during World War II) and brought in top engineering talent to oversee every drawing generated by a young team working long hours.[29] This resilience paid its first dividend in November 1989 when COBE successfully lifted off into space, but the most significant reward was yet to come. In 2006, Mather and George Smoot, principal investigator for one of the spacecraft's instruments, shared a Nobel Prize in Physics for work based on science data from COBE.

Much of the research on resilience has focused on individuals. Since project work happens in team settings, resilience should also be approached from a collective perspective. Team leaders need to anticipate emerging problems and design their team for individual and collective resilience. The research of Kathryn McEwen and Carolyn Boyd identifies the growing importance of team resilience, which is evident in behaviors such as seeking feedback, being cooperative and supportive of each other, and celebrating successes.[30]

Resilience has a strong connection to the concept of a growth mindset identified by Carol Dweck.[31] A growth mindset drives team members to seek out challenging opportunities based on the belief that they can continue to learn and grow. This comfort with growth promotes more resilient behavior in overcoming failure and struggle. It also promotes a team culture of honest feedback, performance review dedicated to continuous improvement, and the development of sustained learning strategies. Organizations such as the US Army and Microsoft have incorporated this concept and diagnostic into their design for successful teams.[32]

Embrace distributed teaming. The highlands and islands of Scotland are among the most beautiful places in the world. They are also very remote: the phrase "you can't get there from here" is particularly applicable to the highlands. This difficult geography has limited economic development in the region, which has driven young people to seek their fortunes elsewhere. In response to this challenge, the Highlands and Islands Enterprise, a government-run economic development organization, sought a way to use the region's natural assets as a magnet to convene creative professionals from around the world for an annual event. This would bring in revenue, and, just as importantly, it would help turn the region into a regular destination for artists and artisans.

Since 2013, the XpoNorth Creative Industries Festival has been doing just that, engaging global talent from sectors ranging from film and music to crafts and publishing. "We needed networks, because the highlands and islands are too small," says Iain Hamilton, cofounder of XpoNorth.[33] Before the COVID-19 pandemic forced a move to an all-digital format, the festival was able to attract 2,000 attendees annually to Inverness, the largest city in the region. From the programming to accommodations and dining, the event planners curated an experience for attendees that made the gathering unique, striving to create a connection that would motivate them to return to the region as part of a creative network.

Hamilton is one of just two civil servants on the XpoNorth team. The rest of the talent needed to plan and execute the events is contracted. This is largely the only way for a government organization to operate with the agility necessary to host a world-class conference of creative talent. "We could move at a speed other government agencies couldn't match, and we had networks they didn't have," says Hamilton.

The XpoNorth approach to teaming, which can be characterized as extremely distributed, is nearly identical to the approach Ed employed throughout his tenure leading the NASA project academy and serving as chief knowledge officer. He and just one deputy ran the project academy for years, occasionally bringing in other civil servants on brief rotational assignments to address specific needs, such as building up the agency's systems engineering capability. Contractors or partners at other NASA centers fulfilled all other functions, from organizing training courses and setting up knowledge-sharing events to providing support for project teams like STEREO.

The primary benefits of extremely distributed teams are speed and flexibility. The abilities to access talent from anywhere and to move quickly when the need arises make it possible to execute a wide range of projects while carrying relatively low overhead. The global pandemic has proved to many businesses what the NASA project academy and XpoNorth already knew: technology has made it possible for project professionals to work with teams around the world. Distributed teams are here to stay.

Putting Teams to Work

People first. Project teams are about people. It sounds simple enough, but in our experience, it is rare for leaders and organizations to think like this. Focus on creating a sense of appreciation and inclusion for team members. Let them know they have an opportunity to do and be part of something special. At the start of a project, take time to acknowledge and introduce all of the team members. Ask them to discuss what they most appreciate about the opportunity to work on the assignment. A short gratitude activity like that can have a powerful impact by reminding team members about the benefits of the journey they are beginning. These conversations also allow team members to identify shared experiences and build rapport quickly.

Growth and learning mindset. Most professional development focuses on the individual. It is a good thing to build individual competence, capability, confidence, and resilience. But since project work is accomplished through team performance, the team should be the unit of measure for learning and knowledge. We have seen numerous teams composed of highly competent practitioners fail spectacularly because they didn't account for the human element of collaboration. One way to ensure this does not happen is to establish a team charter that explicitly identifies growth learning as part of the team's purpose. Team members should be encouraged to plan for their own development and to think about how each project can improve their ability to work effectively in a team setting.

Focus on key goals and outcomes. Teams get frustrated by two things. First, people don't like to be considered "resources," "assets," or "capital." (See "People first" above.) Second, teams get frustrated when they don't know where to focus. A very common plea is for leadership to simply commit to clearly defined priorities. If everything is important, nothing is important.

Just as the critical knowledge process outlined in chapter 1 offers a powerful tool for working with knowledge, it is important to dedicate time and space for quick discussions about the team's mission and progress toward key goals and outcomes. These discussions should be short, unless they are part of a retreat.

Smart and safe failure. No one wants to fail, but there is no way to learn without making mistakes. Successful teams have conversations around acceptable risk, and create conditions for sharing insights from mistakes, mishaps, and failures. Resilience often comes from developing capabilities in response to past failures.

Smart and safe failure means embracing risk-based thinking. A mindset that views risk as a resource will help to counter magical thinking and promote openness to learning from setbacks.

Commitment to purpose. Purpose provides an intrinsic motivation for teams. Research has found that a sense of purpose plays a part in physical and mental health and general well-being.[34] People want to do work that is valued, relevant, and meaningful. Team performance is elevated by a sense of purpose and possibility that points in a clear, if challenging, direction.

We have placed purpose at the end of this list because we consider it the ultimate foundation of a successful team. A team's sense of purpose needs to be refreshed over time. People become complacent. Remind them about the project's purpose in meetings. Find opportunities for team members to present their work and accomplishments so they can explain to others how their work fits into the greater whole. Small acts like this will pay huge dividends: teams that are committed to their purpose will find ways to overcome the most daunting challenges imaginable.

6

Global Collaboration: The International Space Station

Don Cohen

The International Space Station (ISS) may well be the largest, most complex project ever successfully undertaken by international partners. Circling Earth every 90 minutes at an altitude of more than 200 miles, the station is a complex technical marvel. It took 42 flights—37 American and five Russian—to transport its major components for assembly in space over 10 years. It has a mass of nearly 1 million pounds. Components from member countries are joined in a structure that is 357 feet long, and its 16 habitable modules provide living and working space greater than that of a typical six-bedroom home. A 240-foot solar array produces more power than the station needs at any one time, enough to meet the electrical needs of more than 30 homes. The station can dock up to eight spaceships at a time.[1]

Perhaps most impressive is the fact that the design, construction, and operation of the ISS have been a broadly international effort, the close cooperative work of the space agencies and governments of the United States, Russia, Europe, Japan, and Canada. At the time of this writing, the station has been continuously occupied for 21 years; 240 individuals from 19 countries have spent time there. It is not surprising that this hugely ambitious project, which brought together so many agencies and governments (some of them political rivals) and required extremely close and continuous cooperation to succeed, has been nominated for the Nobel Peace prize.

It took years and tireless effort to build that cooperative spirit. The ISS is an example of what Ed, Matt, and Larry referred to in the introduction as a global project. Collaboration was a necessity rather than an option; the challenge was too vast for any one nation to undertake on its own. The need for agreement among a group of international partners made the project inherently political, which meant that political risk was part of the equation. Actual construction began in 1998, but work on the ISS began years before that, with extensive and often difficult planning and negotiation. The foundation for those efforts was laid even earlier, during years of international cooperation on other space projects. Those experiences fostered some of the trust and understanding that the future collaboration required.

The ISS offers important lessons to other large projects, especially those that bring together geographically dispersed and culturally diverse partners. A connected world creates opportunities for international cooperation and sometimes demands it—the COVID-19 pandemic being a case in point. The ISS experience can help guide some of those collaborations. Although few future projects are likely to have the same level of organizational and technical complexity, the successful development of the space station shows how essential it is to any major project to build a sense of shared commitment and understanding through extensive communication, negotiation, and collaborative work.

Another important lesson from the history of the station's success is how thoughtfully project leaders balanced the clear standards needed to build a unified, functional facility with the flexibility needed to respond to unforeseen circumstances and leave room for the preferences and creativity of diverse participating groups. This careful balance exists both in the international agreements that govern responsibilities and expectations and in the design of the station itself.

Foundations

As early as 1980, before the US government officially committed to developing the ISS, NASA began working with the space agencies of Canada, Europe, and Japan to consider how building and using a shared space station would work: what each agency's hardware contributions would be, and how the complex issues of finances and management would be handled. Lyn Wigbels, who led NASA's internal process of developing a potential agreement for the design, development, and operation of a station, knew the plan would need to respect the needs of all partner agencies and governments to have any chance of acceptance. One key to the success of this difficult process was involving all interested parties from the beginning. That gave the partners a chance to understand one another's positions and, in effect, to develop a strategy together rather than respond to a detailed set of demands independently devised by another agency.

As the biggest player by far and the one with the most experience in space technology, NASA needed to learn to be open to other agencies' interests and ways of working. That was one aspect of a complex process that demanded time and patience. Many bilateral and multilateral discussions and numerous drafts were needed to arrive at decisions that all involved agencies and governments could agree on. Wigbels notes that two provisions—agreeing that partners would try to minimize the exchange of funds (instead using the barter of services whenever possible) and giving partners the right to use their own transportation systems—were key to finding agreements. The fact that these negotiations began before station development was officially a project made it possible to do this work without the pressure of a construction schedule.[2]

Negotiations with the Russians, which began in the 1990s, presented special challenges since the Russians and the United States had long been rivals in both politics and space technology. The first steps in developing trust and understanding between groups that have not previously worked together are the hardest. The parties need at least a presumption of trustworthiness and common purpose to willingly undertake the joint work that can foster greater mutual confidence.

Where might that basis for collaboration come from? A long process of working together on official negotiations can gradually build the necessary confidence. Shared professional competence is also an important source of trust and respect. Engineers and others in related technical fields earn one another's respect by displaying knowledge of their craft; they are, in effect, members of an informal community of practice, even when they live and work in different countries and have not previously been acquainted. They stand together on the common ground of a particular technical discipline. Another source of cooperative effort is demonstrated commitment to a clearly defined shared goal, proof that your partners are working toward the same important end that you are. Some confidence that your future partners want what you want is essential from the beginning. This sense of mutuality must be demonstrated and strengthened again and again during the course of the project.

William Gerstenmaier's experience in Russia provides an example of fostering the trust and understanding the ISS work would need. In 1995 and 1996, he spent six months in Russia as ground liaison for NASA astronaut Shannon Lucid during her time on Mir, the Russian space station that preceded the ISS. Gerstenmaier had an opportunity to show the Russians his technical knowledge and his commitment to the work. In an interview with NASA's *ASK Magazine*, he explained:[3]

> I was the first American to go to Russia as an ops lead in charge of
> [Lucid's] science program and stay there for an extended period of
> time. Prior to that, folks would come for a couple of weeks, then
> they would go back to the U.S. and another person would come.
> I was the first person that stayed the entire time (approximately six
> months). . . . And because I had background on shuttle and station
> and propulsion, I wasn't the typical science person that's fresh
> out of school. I actually had a lot of experience in short-duration
> spaceflight that the Russians were not used to seeing.

The Russians witnessed Gerstenmaier's respect for technical realities. He knew from first-hand knowledge of the Russian program that some of NASA's negotiating points were infeasible, so in conversations with his counterparts he would simply scrap those requests. "They [the Russians] weren't used to having someone on the other side of the table who was knowledgeable enough." Respect for Gerstenmaeier's expertise and a shared commitment to making things work formed the basis for a stronger, more trusting relationship. As the Russians got to know him, and he got to know them, he would sit in the back of the room and listen in on teleconferences with NASA. "They would go to me and say, 'This is crazy. You know we can't do this.' I actually got to see what a NASA-American looks like to a Russian through their cultural eyes." When Gerstenmaier later became NASA's deputy program manager for the space station, these relationships paid off: "I know these folks personally; I've worked with them; I lived in their country. They know me. I know their culture."

In addition to Lucid's nearly six-month stay on the Russian station, NASA sent supplies to Mir, including some American scientific instruments—an early example of the multinational science work that would define the ISS. This collaboration, which stemmed from a July 1991 agreement signed by President George H. W. Bush and Soviet leader Mikhail Gorbachev, continued under Boris Yeltsin's leadership of the Russian Federation after the dissolution of the Soviet Union.[4] There were seven Shuttle-Mir EVAs (extravehicular activities), and astronauts from each country trained at the other country's facility.[5]

US-Russian cooperation on Mir was an essential precursor to joint work on the ISS. John McBrine, who served three tours at Russia's astronaut training center at Star City, including as director of operations for NASA, says the NASA/Mir program "polished" NASA's relationship with the Russian space agency. The relationship was strengthened by collaborating and coming to understand and respect one another's ways of getting things done. McBrine learned that the Russians have "a different mindset, a different way of working." Over time, he got to know "who makes things happen and how to make things happen," and the importance of personal relationships in getting work done. He notes that those personal relationships provide a degree of transparency that might not be available through official channels. Engineers talking to engineers focus on shared technical issues, not national differences. As McBrine says, "a 90° angle is a 90° angle."[6]

A dangerous fire aboard MIR in 1997 tested and proved the quality of the relationship between the two countries. One American astronaut, Jerry Linenger, was part of the crew when a Russian oxygen-generating canister malfunctioned, filling the spacecraft with acrid smoke. The crew managed to control the fire, and Linenger, a physician, checked his fellow astronauts to make sure none had been injured. In the months that followed, NASA and the Russian space agency worked together to develop a safer canister and create shielding that would prevent a future fire from spreading. Harold Beeson, a NASA expert on materials flammability in high-oxygen conditions, explained the importance of working to develop a collaborative relationship with the Russians: "There was a delicate political balance to maintain. You didn't want to be the ugly American that's standing back and saying, 'You had a failed system.' We wanted to make sure that we could build the team that was trying to solve this problem, with everybody's focus on the problem and not on assigning blame."[7] In this context, simple efforts to build cohesion like regularly having lunch together helped bring the teams together. The improved, safer oxygen generators that resulted from the collaboration are used on the ISS.

Cady Coleman, a NASA astronaut who spent six months on the ISS in 2010 and 2011 as part of crews consisting mainly of Americans and Russians, sums up the personal connection that makes working together possible when she says understanding the language and culture of others is a sign of recognition and respect, a way of saying "I see you."[8]

Negotiation and Agreement

As the early history of preliminary ISS work suggests, a critical lesson for other large, culturally and geographically dispersed projects is that the necessary planning and negotiation take a lot of time and thoughtful diplomatic effort. Rushing to get to the "real work" is a potentially fatal error. Those early stages provide an essential foundation that will support the final structure.

Lynn Cline, chief NASA negotiator of the ISS agreement with Russia, notes that those negotiations took four long years to accomplish. "The invitation to the Russians to join the partnership officially was issued in 1993," she says, "and I guess it was '97 when the negotiations were finally completed. Then the language of the negotiations had to be verified and so on. It was early '98 when the signing ceremony was held."[9] It would be difficult to overstate the complexity of the negotiations. Although the conversations were bilateral—between NASA and the Russian space agency—they needed the agreement of all the partner agencies. Cline says:

> If Europe asked for changes, I would have to convey them in turn
> to Canada, Japan, and Russia and get all those countries to agree
> before I could agree to them. In the end, even though there are

separate bilateral agreements, there are certain provisions that have
to be identical across the board because you can't have five different
management approaches. Since we were meeting bilaterally, it
was a highly iterative process. You had to come back to the same
points over and over. How many rounds do you have to go before
everyone is on board for the same compromise for that particular
provision? It was very time consuming.

NASA's original partners—Canada, Europe, and Japan—were under-
standably nervous that they would lose rights and obligations by
bringing in Russia. Although the political rivalries of the Cold War
had ebbed, the partners had to be convinced that bringing the Russian space agency's significant capabilities into the partnership would
be good for everyone. Cline says, "I could tell the Russians, 'Gee, I'd
accommodate you but then I'd lose the Europeans.' Or 'the Japanese
can't change.' . . . It was a challenge to understand what were the real
issues and what were negotiating tactics." Adding to the complexity was the fact that five governments, not just their space agencies,
necessarily had a voice in the negotiations. Cline notes, "I was one of
the NASA representatives to the intergovernmental agreement negotiations. That was a State Department–led political multilateral agreement above the space agency level memoranda of understanding."

Cline had the background and skills her difficult job demanded.
A foreign-language major in college, she first worked on US-Soviet
affairs when she interned at NASA and participated in the follow-
up to the Apollo-Soyuz Test Project, the first space collaboration
between the United States and the Soviet Union. Later, she led US
delegations to the United Nations Committee on the Peaceful Uses
of Outer Space. Equally important, she had the personal skills a successful negotiator needs:

The comment that people have made to me many times over my
career is that I'm a very good listener. I think because I majored
in a foreign language and learned that other countries say things
differently, you think differently when you don't have identical
words for saying things, and I've always been interested in other

cultures. I can put myself in other people's shoes. I've also been told I have the patience of Job. I can have the same discussion 20 times and not blow my top. All of those are essential in negotiations.[10]

This is another key lesson for global projects: success depends on hiring people who have the cultural and relationship skills needed to foster agreement and cooperation, not just people with the necessary technical expertise. Like Gerstenmaier, Cline emphasizes the importance of personal relationships in arriving at a workable agreement. While NASA often had turnover in its personnel, the Russians employed veterans of the Apollo-Soyuz program who remembered working successfully with Americans. It was a lesson that NASA had to learn from experience, according to Cline:

> At the beginning JSC [Johnson Space Center] would rotate people through and send a different avionics expert or a different structural expert the next time, and the Russians didn't know how to deal with that, because they knew the other guy. They'd finally just gotten to know him. "Who's this guy that we don't know?" JSC learned that you had to respect that personal relationship. If you were going to change out people, then the original guy who'd built up the relationships needed to personally introduce his successor and say, "I vouch for him, he's really good, and please work with him the same way you did with me."[11]

NASA was not always perfect in its collaborative efforts on the station. In a July 2011 conversation that Ed moderated between Kuniaki Shiraki of the Japanese Space Exploration Agency (JAXA) and Gerstenmaier, Shiraki spoke frankly about the difficulties of the partnership in the 1980s, noting that as a smaller agency with less experience in space, JAXA had to "fight with NASA" for a time before eventually establishing a good working relationship.[12]

Building those trusting relationships was essential. Cline points to flexibility as a critical element of success, because of both the variety and complexity of partner needs and the fact that a long-term project will necessarily face changes and surprises. "One of the things you need to avoid as a negotiator is getting *too* precise because things change, especially on a long-term program," she says. "Technical issues will arise; the policies of governments will change; administrations will change. I think these agreements have been remarkably flexible."[13]

Workable flexibility in operations and management depends on clearly distinguishing between bedrock principles that must be followed to avoid chaos and the areas where rigid adherence to detailed rules is unnecessarily restrictive and counterproductive. The same is true of the negotiated physical design of the station. Many elements must be rigorously standardized, such as hardware that connects parts of the station built by different countries and provides essential services, and the docking system to accommodate spacecraft from different countries. The most impressive evidence of the success of this technological coordination is the fact that the ISS's modules, constructed in different countries by different space agencies, were seamlessly connected more than 200 miles above Earth. Beyond the necessary constraints, however, station design allows for variation that enables agencies to use technologies they have developed and valued over time. NASA and Russian modules have some different capabilities and technologies including, for instance, different ways of producing supplemental oxygen.

Granting partners the freedom to make their own choices in response to unforeseen circumstances depends on trusting their good sense and good will—in other words, on having established a good working relationship. When trust is lacking, everything has to be spelled out. Cline says, "That [relationship] was far more important than anything written on a piece of paper," and points out that, "If going forward with this program with your counterpart requires you to rely on detailed language, you've got a communication and relationship problem."[14] Although the length of negotiations with the Russians must have been frustrating in many ways, those many long months of working together strengthened the relationships that made agreement possible. "We started out fighting over principles that we thought were going to be really important, but once people start working together and build trust and respect for one another, they figure out how to work together without having to go back to chapter and verse of the agreement and insist on what it says in Article 4, Chapter 3," says Cline.[15] "It just becomes people working together who have a common goal."

That last point is critical. Unless the teams are working toward a common result clearly understood and valued by all, no amount of mutual trust and respect will create the necessary coordination.

Maintaining Project Knowledge Over Time

A challenge for large, multiyear projects is preserving essential knowledge in an accessible and usable form. Over time, some of the developers of project technologies are likely to move on or retire, potentially taking their deep understanding of their work with them—subtleties of how things work that need to be known to complete the project successfully.

Large, innovative projects are engines of knowledge creation. In addition to having that knowledge available for their own use and reuse, the projects can become important resources for future work, provided that their knowledge is carefully preserved and effectively shared. This does not happen nearly as often as it should. Tight schedules, limited human and financial resources, and the fact that curating knowledge is seldom anyone's official job often mean that knowledge disappears.

The International Space Station project included some knowledge retention measures that have proved their value over time. Tim Howell, a former ISS engineer, worked on Design Knowledge Capture (DKC), an initiative started in late 1997 to create a repository of real-world knowledge about elements of station design. The initiative was a response to the certainty that some or much of that mainly tacit knowledge would be lost over the possible thirty-year life of the station if nothing were done to preserve it. Howell quotes a NASA ISS program manager who explains, "I don't want to call a console operator to ask how long a Remote Power Control Module will last before it fails and get an answer quoted from a spec document on that person's computer. I want that console operator to tell me what the real design margins are based on what he or she has learned from the person who designed it."[16]

Howell says, "With limited time and resources, we focused on identifying key experts before they left the program. With the help of team managers and coworkers, we were on a mission to find ISS subject matter experts who were identified by their peers as the most knowledgeable in their engineering disciplines." "Capture, Index, Share" was the initiative's slogan. Contacts at organizations involved in ISS design directed the DKC team to subject matter experts, especially the ones about to retire or join other programs. Discussions that focused on the essentials of how things actually work were video-recorded and the content indexed by topic on the DKC website so engineers could easily find what they needed.

Sometimes the knowledge identified led immediately to new procedures and training protocols. For instance, solar panel designers knew that storage of the folded panels could cause them to stick together, or that surface tension might cause cables involved in deployment in space to jump off their pulleys. Given this information, the astronaut office and solar array design engineers created a new cable-retraction tool and slowed the deployment process to reduce surface tension effects.

The DKC team spent eight hours with a designer of an EVA airlock system, interviewing him and videotaping his tour of the airlock being assembled at his facility. A few months later, the engineer left the company. In many organizations, his departure would have meant a damaging loss of knowledge about the how and why of the system. The DKC initiative work avoided that common problem.

Cooperation in Action

The cooperative spirit fostered during pre-ISS joint work, years of ISS negotiations, and station construction has characterized the successful collaboration of the multinational crews that have worked on the station for more than two decades. Shared work and familiarity with one another's languages and cultures have fostered personal relationships of trust, respect, and openness to learning from other approaches to the work. That trust and respect serve as a foundation that enables flexibility to do what needs to be done in pursuit of shared goals rather than strict adherence to a set of rules.

Some of that cooperation takes the form of mutually beneficial technology exchange. The Russians, who did not have lights on their spacesuits and could not work outside the station during night passes, adapted their suits to accommodate American-made lights. The Americans have adapted their helmet cameras to fit Russian spacesuits. Russian brass ties are widely used by other crew members to tie down cables. "There's been a tremendous amount of learning on both sides," says Gerstenmaier. "I think that's the wave of the future."[17]

Gerstenmaier believes that working together is especially important to knowledge transfer across cultures:

> The cultures are so different that if I just gave them a report, they wouldn't understand it with the same cultural mindset that I have. But when you physically see it work, you see it through your own cultural lens and your own activity, so adaptation and absorption are quicker. In diverse cultural environments, demonstrating a capability is more effective than academic proof that a concept or a device works.

Coleman notes that the crews on the ISS are just "the tip of the iceberg" of people involved in station operations. Ground crews in member countries are continually monitoring, supporting, and directing activity on the station, and they, too, experience the effects and benefits of international cooperation. During her time on the station in 2009, NASA astronaut Nicole Stott participated in the first successful docking of a Japanese cargo vehicle sent to the ISS. Later, on a trip to Japan, she visited the Japanese mission control center for the station. As soon as she entered the room, everyone stood and bowed to her to show their gratitude for her work—an unforgettable moment of international connection and appreciation.[18]

Successful collaboration often depends on the informal personal relationships that develop between participants. Coleman describes an interaction with the Russians in the late 1990s: She was given the job of negotiating with them to put English-language labels on equipment in the Russian segment of the station as a way to avoid potential confusion about their functions. Her initial request, to add English labels to everything the crew would touch, was turned down, so she asked if they could label everything the crew would touch "a lot." That request was also denied, as was her suggestion that they label everything the crew would have to replace or maintain. The Russians, adamant, insisted, "Nothing will need to be replaced." Their refusal seemed final and absolute, but when Coleman talked to these same people during a smoking break (she didn't smoke herself but valued the opportunity to have informal conversations), the results were very different. When she asked why they didn't want to label the equipment, they explained, "The panels are already made, engraved in Russian." When she suggested they add overlays in both languages, they told her they couldn't make overlays. These admissions of limited budgets or capabilities wouldn't have been made during the more formal negotiation. Once Coleman understood what the real issue was, she could assure them that NASA would make the overlays. The problem was solved.

Discussing the solution for another problem, that of excessive noise from fans and pumps on the station, Coleman again emphasized the importance of personal relationships: "You need acoustics experts to work with the Russians and you need the personal connection that says, 'I *see* you, and we're doing this work together.' You do that with dinner and remembering that someone has grandkids."

Managing the Unforeseen

Any project that has a long life will encounter unexpected challenges and possibly unanticipated opportunities. Because it is impossible to plan for every possible contingency, having the freedom to respond to novel situations in novel ways is essential. As suggested, that flexibility has two sources: avoiding rigidity in procedures and regulations that would inhibit new approaches, and building strong working relationships that encourage mutual aid and entrust partners to act responsibly. Those strengths have served the ISS well in large and small ways.

The *Columbia* disaster of 2003 grounded the space shuttle program until mid-2005 while NASA studied the cause of the accident and developed strategies to avoid a similar problem in the future. During that time, Russia's Soyuz spacecraft offered the only available access to the station. The response to that unexpected change went smoothly because of the good relationship the Americans and Russians had developed over time. "We had almost ten years of working with the Russians before *Columbia*. When *Columbia* occurred, we were going to have to use the Soyuz on a routine basis," says Gerstenmaier. "But you couldn't immediately have gone to that dependence and interaction without some lower-level, non-risky interaction that built confidence before the crisis. You almost have to stage the relationship such that you learn and gain this trust."[19]

Ongoing Benefits

It is difficult to pinpoint the end of the ISS's useful life. Aging technology means it cannot go on indefinitely, but the decision of when to stop supporting it is political as well as technical. At this point, discussions about a transition to commercial support of the station are inconclusive. It seems likely, though, that the ISS will continue to operate at least until the mid-2020s, continuing to conduct valuable science and strengthen ties among its partners.

Both in the next few years and even after the ISS is no longer operating, it will continue to provide important benefits. Just as pre-ISS collaboration helped make cooperation on the space station possible, the decades of joint work on the station have provided the foundation for other international efforts. Given the enormous expense of space exploration and the breadth of technical demands, future ambitious exploration programs will necessarily be international efforts. Results of some of the research done on the ISS—especially on how to maintain astronauts' bone health and strength during prolonged periods of microgravity—will be essential to future human exploration beyond Earth's orbit. And the International Project/Programme Management Committee (IPMC), founded in 2010 under the umbrella of the International Astronautical Federation, would not have been formed without the ISS, which established the connections used to form the committee and demonstrated the possibilities of international cooperation. The IPMC has supported the foundation of an international project management course facilitated by the NASA project academy that brings engineers from various space agencies together to learn and build relationships.[20]

Another benefit of the ISS is that it has served as a training ground for a new generation of professionals who have had the opportunity to learn from its founders and then make their own contributions. Although space agencies are always striving to do new things, their successful innovations always have deep roots in knowledge gained, preserved, and communicated in the past.

Lessons Learned: No Shortcuts on the Road to Success

The ISS offers lessons to planners and builders of other complex cooperative projects. As clear and important as those lessons are, the ubiquitous pressure for speed and efficiency and reluctance to invest in soft skills make them hard to implement. Success is likely to depend on overcoming that resistance.

Invest time and effort in establishing mutual trust and understanding among participants. Organizations driven to get things done as quickly as possible are in danger of shortchanging this critical step. Without essential planning, negotiation, and relationship building, efforts to hit the ground running will lead to painful stumbles.

Hire people with relationship skills. The process of relationship-building recognizes that a lot of good work gets done through informal networks of relationships known as social capital. The ISS story is full of examples of problems solved and agreements reached thanks to personal connections developed between participants during the process of working together toward a shared goal. That process also shows the importance of having people with the relationship skills needed to foster agreement; their absence would be at least as damaging to the project as not having all the necessary technical skill.

Face-to-face communication matters. Much of the coordination of dispersed work happens remotely, using the increasingly sophisticated and reliable collaboration tools now available. But critical aspects of complex projects demand rich dialogue, subtle understanding, and trust that are only possible when people are physically together at work and in social settings. Difficult negotiations, key decision-making, responses to crises, and analysis of ambiguous information all call for in-person collaboration. The history of the ISS shows the benefits of being together again and again. Similar examples are provided by the high-energy physics experiments at CERN, which, like the station, is a long-duration, innovative, ambitious international project. Much of CERN's collaboration has taken place virtually, but scientists and engineers have invariably met in person for critical negotiation and planning and to evaluate complex results.

Involve everyone early. Part of achieving agreement and commitment is bringing all players to the table from the beginning and giving them a voice in planning and development. That early participation creates a sense of ownership and commitment that would be much harder to come by if plans were presented to teams as a fait accompli, a set of orders to be carried out.

Build in flexibility. The history of the station also makes clear the importance of flexibility in negotiation, planning, and operation. Any project that has a long life is going to run into challenges and opportunities that cannot be addressed by a rigid set of rules. People need sufficient autonomy to deal with the unexpected.

Flexibility also leaves room for the various teams to make unique contributions to the project. One of the benefits of bringing together participants from diverse cultures is the opportunity to take advantage of their different skills and perspectives. That variety increases the project's repertoire of approaches to solving problems. Cultural differences can be assets. Too much emphasis on control and standardization stifles creativity.

Focus on the purpose. Spend time ensuring that all participants understand the aim of the work and share a commitment to achieving the goal. Keeping the shared goal visible throughout the project helps overcome conflicts and problems that are likely to arise.

Most of these lessons point to one important underlying truth: establishing connection, understanding, and commitment is not a one-time task; it is a continuous process that remains essential for the whole life of a project.

7
The Way Forward:
Mission-Critical Advice

Nothing is so painful to the human mind as a great and sudden change.

—Mary Shelley, *Frankenstein*

When Ed was growing up in Brooklyn, his school would take class trips to the beach every year. Before he learned to swim, he found the power of the ocean threatening, and he dreaded going on these trips. But one thing that stuck with him from those experiences was practical advice about what to do in the event of a riptide: don't fight it. Swim parallel to the shoreline until you're outside its grip. Decades later, this lesson came to mind when he found himself caught in a riptide in the Hamptons. After an initial wave of panic, he let the water carry him where it wanted rather than trying to resist its force. He wound up on a beach a mile from where he'd started, exhausted and grateful for the knowledge that had saved his life.

Many of the project professionals we have taught or consulted with in recent years can relate to the metaphor of swimming in a riptide. We are living in a time characterized by *radical uncertainty*, which John Kay and Mervyn King define as "the vast range

of possibilities that lie in between the world of unlikely events . . .
and the world of the unimaginable."[1] We write this in late 2020 amid
a global pandemic that has upended the status quo ante in unanticipated ways. The pandemic is only the latest and greatest reminder
that radical uncertainty requires new ways of thinking.

Turbulence and Risk

In a world of radical uncertainty, the biggest risks to projects are social,
political, and economic. Events ranging from Brexit to COVID-19
have exposed more than the vulnerability of global supply chains—
they have illuminated cracks along fault lines where tectonic plates
collide. Projects that demand the kind of sustained international
cooperation that was necessary to design, build, and operate the
International Space Station are harder to establish when forces such
as nationalism strain relations among countries that both compete
and collaborate. The pandemic-induced shift to remote and virtual
work has vast implications for the way project teams work and learn
together. The future of commercial real estate construction in the
world's major cities is now an open question. These are just a few
examples of the political, social, and economic risks on the horizon of
the project world today. The only sure thing is that there will be others tomorrow.

Technology contributes to radical uncertainty because the velocity of change makes it nearly impossible to predict which trends will
accelerate most rapidly. The unforeseen move to remote and virtual
work in 2020 created an overnight demand for secure, reliable communication tools at a scale that was previously unimaginable. Based
on recent trends in project work, it is reasonable to expect that artificial intelligence (AI) and machine learning will be employed for
increasingly complex pattern recognition tasks, just as robots will

continue to take over work that is physically demanding, dangerous, or repetitive. These technologies introduce new risks and raise
ethical and epistemic concerns that need to be addressed through a
humanistic lens.

We are not futurologists, and the mercurial nature of social and
political risks makes us leery of predictions about the state of the
world in two or five years. (Consider how many political experts dis-
counted both Trump and Biden in the early stages of their respective
campaigns that led to victory.[2]) But we are confident that a landscape
contoured by radical uncertainty has significant implications for
knowledge and leadership.

Knowledge

One result of radical uncertainty is *epistemic* uncertainty. All knowledge is temporal. A physicist working at the turn of the twentieth century could scarcely have imagined that the laws of classical mechanics
would not hold at the quantum level. What works for today may not
work for tomorrow, and this is particularly true as the velocity of
change increases.

The need for speed. The relationship between the rate of change
and the speed of thought required to respond leads us to a rule of
thumb about the likelihood of relying on habits of thought ingrained
by heuristics and cognitive biases. There is a direct relationship
between the rapidity of human decision-making and the use of mental shortcuts that introduce predictable errors. The faster the pace, the
more tempting it is to lean on familiar patterns that reduce friction.
Information that is easily recalled isn't always the most relevant. A
story that reduces the complexity of an issue may lead to simplistic
conclusions. The usual suspects should not be expected to think differently than they always do. The only answer for the trap of fast

thinking is slow thinking: deliberation, conversation, and reflection. A decision maker who doesn't pause to ask questions about biases, risks, or misinformation is a dead man walking.

$$v = P\ (b)$$

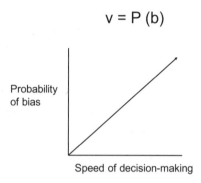

Stopping the clock is not always possible, but our experience is that too often the *perceived* need for speed shapes the decision-making reality. In 2003, a contractor team working six days a week on a weather satellite project for NASA neglected to secure the satellite to a cart with the proper number of bolts before moving it, resulting in a mishap that cost $135 million to repair.[3] The project was not scheduled to launch for years—there was no reason the team needed to be working on a weekend. Speed had become a goal unto itself, leading to a failure to ask the obvious question ("Are we doing things right?"), to say nothing of the one that a learning organization routinely asks ("Are we doing the right things?"). Radical uncertainty only increases the importance of making time for the latter question.

Learning and unlearning. Uncertainty about the knowledge that will be needed in the future means that continuous learning is now a sink-or-swim proposition for project professionals at all career levels. Digital transformation of processes, business models, and product lines demands increased capacity for managing change in addition to technical skill. AI won't replace managers, but managers who use AI will replace those who don't.[4] While skill gaps need to be addressed, the human dynamics of digital transformation require something more difficult: unlearning what has worked in the past in order to enable experimentation that can lead to breakthroughs.[5]

But keeping up with technology is simply the price of admission. The longer-term challenge is to read, listen, and gain exposure to a wide range of topics in order to think broadly and holistically. Just as STEM (science, technology, engineering, and mathematics) education has moved in the direction of STEAM (the *A* stands for arts), the value of multidisciplinary learning throughout a career has begun to receive due recognition. This wider lens enables practitioners to avoid relying on old patterns of thought that are no longer useful.[6]

If this sounds like yet another angst-inducing item for the to-do list, there is good news on that front as well: learning does more than just making us smarter. Current research on coping with the pressures of work suggests that learning leads to reduced feelings of distress and anxiety and is a powerful tool for building resilience. The creation of new knowledge prepares us for dealing with challenges, threats, and change.[7]

Teams and organizations have the same need to refresh their knowledge. As projects continue to increase in complexity, inclusion can serve as a deliberate strategy for seeking out new ideas. The Netflix Challenge mentioned in chapter 5 is an example of casting the widest possible net, but inclusion can start closer to home. Psychological safety enables team members to share ideas freely without risk of recrimination. As a team bonds and finds its working rhythm, however, the importance of cohesion has to be balanced against the risk of creating a culture of exclusion that communicates the message that outside ideas are neither needed nor welcome. As NASA discovered with the *Challenger* accident, that road leads to hubris and failure.

Judgment and ethics. A machine can run numbers faster than any human, but it cannot ask or answer questions like "Do these numbers look right?" or "Are these the right numbers?" The answers to those questions require judgment. Judgment encompasses the ability to

understand context, separate signal from noise, weigh ethical considerations, and exercise emotional intelligence and sensitivity.[8] These
are all critical abilities, yet very little education or training focuses on
how to develop and exercise this skill.

As artificial intelligence and machine learning become increasingly integrated in project work, they come with risks that are still
emerging. AI can create increasingly sophisticated fakes of everything
from human images to news stories. Machine learning can generate
biased outcomes as a result of bias-ridden data, faulty algorithms,
or a combination of the two. The work of sorting through these
and other unforeseen challenges will fall to people who will need to
be trained as thoroughly in ethics as in technology. New knowledge
will be needed to develop more discerning judgment when assessing
the quality and value of work produced by machines.

As we write this, Google has established a low-cost certification for
information technology professionals that provides highly transferable
skills in some of the most common computer languages in use today.[9]
At first blush, this sounds like a wonderful gift that can help to level
the playing field in a deeply unequal society. But it quickly raises questions about the educational priorities of a tech firm with a market capi-
talization of $1 trillion. What aspects of ethics and social responsibility
will be taught? Where will judgment and contextual thinking fit into
the curriculum? How will a workforce trained by and for a private sec-
tor firm that owns some of the most powerful algorithms in the world
learn to make decisions that have consequences for billions of people?

Leadership

How does one lead in a landscape of radical uncertainty? Leaders are
expected to be able to define reality and mobilize resources.[10] The dif-
ficulty begins with the first part of that proposition: reality is temporal and fragmented.

While the lure of technology is strong, attempts to build a higher-fidelity dashboard representation of reality are the equivalent of trying to capture lightning in a bottle. Access to critical real-time data is essential, but it is a category error to mistake curated data for reality. Leading organizations through radical uncertainty is not the same as piloting an aircraft through foul weather. It's not possible to rely on instruments to hit the middle of the runway 99.9 percent of the time.

There is an alternative to trying to define reality through technology: abandon the control paradigm. Hire people you can trust and give them the decision authority to do their jobs at the local level. Provide the learning and knowledge infrastructure they need, and focus on intangibles such as teamwork, collaboration, and culture. Let them sense and respond to the various realities they encounter. Communicate transparently and hold them accountable for results.

Radical uncertainty does not mean there is no role for strategy. One part of defining reality that is reserved for leaders is grappling with political and social risks that may be unevenly distributed across geographies. In the United States today, for instance, section 230 of the Communications Decency Act of 1996 is a political hot potato for some of the world's largest tech companies. Section 230 currently protects companies that own social media platforms from legal liability for the content posted by users on those sites, even if the information posted is misleading or false. A change to this would have potentially enormous consequences for the US operations of YouTube, Facebook, Twitter, and other social media companies. Now consider how the same challenges might play out in a hundred or more countries, each with their own legal and regulatory frameworks, and the need for a strategic perspective becomes evident. Similarly, the pandemic has laid bare the risk posed by worker health in global supply chains. Understanding and navigating risks like these can only be done at the macro level.

Though the responsibility for exercising judgment with regard to technology is shared by many, ultimate accountability rests with leaders. This much seems clear: problems with technical solutions will increasingly be solved by machines. The ethical and epistemic questions will only get harder as technology proliferates, and bedrock questions such as "Are we doing the right things?" will become more important. AI and machine learning will continue to tackle tasks that were once thought to be the exclusive province of technical experts (just ask any radiologist), but the social problems inherent in teamwork, collaboration, and organizational culture will always come down to people.

If we have emphasized one theme throughout this book, it is that focusing on the human dimension of project work offers the greatest potential for return on investment to an organization, its stakeholders, and society. As we said in the introduction, projects run on knowledge that can be technical, organizational, or political. Teams function within organizations that empower or constrain them through a combination of bureaucratic means such as governance and intangibles such as culture and a shared sense of mission and purpose. They explore, fail, improvise, and maneuver in response to challenges they didn't or couldn't anticipate, and as a result they learn the only way they can: together. The starting point for knowledge is not information. It is people.

Notes

Introduction

1. Arie de Geus, "Planning as Learning," *Harvard Business Review* 66, no. 2 (March–April 1988): 70–74, https://hbr.org/1988/03/planning-as-learning.

2. Rick Waghorn, "Distance Learning," *Project* (February 2009), 12–14, https://www.nasa.gov/pdf/321075main_Project_Magazine_excerpt.pdf.

Chapter 1

1. During Ed's tenure at NASA, the organization he led that focused on building project management capability evolved and went by different names. For the sake of simplicity, we refer to all of these as "the NASA project academy" throughout the book.

2. Naoki Ogiwara, email correspondence with Laurence Prusak, December 20, 2020.

3. Robert Gibbons and Laurence Prusak, "Knowledge, Stories, and Culture in Organizations," *AEA Papers and Proceedings* 110 (2020):187–192, https://doi.org/10.1257/pandp.20201091.

4. H. E. Sana Mohamad Suhail, interview by the authors, December 24, 2020.

5. NASA Academy of Program/Project & Engineering Leadership, "Collaborative Problem-Solving: The STS-119 Flow Control Valve Issue," NASA, April 2013, https://appel.nasa.gov/wp-content/uploads/2013/04/468375main_STS-119_flow_control_valve.pdf.

6. Gabriel Szulanski, *Sticky Knowledge: Barriers to Knowing in the Firm* (London: SAGE Publications, 2003), 2.

7. Ray Ryan, interview by the authors, August 23, 2020.

8. Ikujiro Nonaka and Noboru Konno, "The Concept of '*Ba*': Building a Foundation for Knowledge Creation," *California Management Review* 40, no. 3 (Spring 1988): 40–54, https://home.business.utah.edu/actme/7410/Nonaka%201998.pdf.

9. "Novartis Campus 2010," *Architecture and Urbanism* (November 2010), https://au-magazine.com/shop/architecture-and-urbanism/au-201011/.

10. Steven Levy, "Apple's New Campus: An Exclusive Look Inside the Mothership," *Wired*, May 16, 2017, https://www.wired.com/2017/05/apple-park-new-silicon-valley-campus/.

11. Gretchen Gavett, "Think Carefully about Where You Put the Office Bathroom," *Harvard Business Review* (July 2013), https://hbr.org/2013/07/think-carefully-about-where-yo.

12. Ethan S. Bernstein and Stephen Turban, "The Impact of the 'Open' Workspace on Human Collaboration," *Philosophical Transactions of the Royal Society B* (July 2, 2018), https://doi.org/10.1098/rstb.2017.0239. For more on this, see also Libby Sander, "A New Study Should Be the Final Nail for Open-Plan Offices," *The Conversation*, July 17, 2018, https://theconversation.com/a-new-study-should-be-the-final-nail-for-open-plan-offices-99756; and Sunanda Creagh, "Open Plan Offices Attract Highest Levels of Worker Dissatisfaction: Study," *The Conversation*, September 16, 2013, https://theconversation.com/open-plan-offices-attract-highest-levels-of-worker-dissatisfaction-study-18246.

13. Thomas H. Davenport and Laurence Prusak, *Working Knowledge: How Organizations Manage What They Know* (Boston: Harvard Business School Press, 1998), 7. See also Richard F. Meyer, Michael G. Rukstad, Peter J. Coughlan, and Stephan A. Jansen, "DaimlerChrysler Post-Merger Integration," Case, Harvard Business Publishing, last revised December 1, 2005, https://hbsp.harvard.edu/product/703417-PDF-ENG.

14. David J. Teece, Gary Pisano, and Amy Shuen, "Dynamic Capabilities and Strategic Management," *Strategic Management Journal* 18, no. 7 (August 1997): 509–533.

15. Robert Gibbons, correspondence with Laurence Prusak, December 20, 2020.

16. John Maynard Keynes, *The General Theory of Employment, Interest and Money* (1936; repr., London: Palgrave Macmillan, 2018).

17. Al Jacobson and Laurence Prusak, "The Cost of Knowledge," *Harvard Business Review* 84, no. 11 (November 2006), https://hbr.org/2006/11/the-cost-of-knowledge.

18. Thomas H. Davenport, R. G. Eccles, and Laurence Prusak, "Information Politics," *Sloan Management Review* 34, no. 1 (1992): 53–65.

19. NASA Academy of Program/Project & Engineering Leadership, "Young Professionals Brief: The Next Generation on Knowledge," *ASK the Academy* 6, no. 1 (January 31, 2013), https://appel.nasa.gov/2013/01/31/6-1_yp_nextgen_knowledge-html/.

Chapter 2

1. For more about the "Faster, Better, Cheaper" era at NASA, see Howard E. McCurdy, *Faster, Better, Cheaper: Low-Cost Innovation in the U.S. Space Program* (Baltimore, MD: Johns Hopkins Press, 2001).

2. This learning model, which Ed first presented at NASA in 1984, is based on the work of David Kolb. See David A. Kolb, *Experiential Learning: Experience as the Source of Learning and Development* (Englewood Cliffs, NJ: Prentice-Hall, 1984).

3. Education Development Center, *The Teaching Firm: Where Productive Work and Learning Converge. Report on Research Findings and Implications* (Newton, MA: Education Development Center, 1998), 9, https://files.eric.ed.gov/fulltext/ED461754.pdf.

4. Katie Smith Milway and Amy Saxton, "The Challenge of Organizational Learning," *Stanford Social Innovation Review* 9, no. 3 (Summer 2011): 44–49.

5. Chipotle has retrained its employees more than once. See Elizabeth Chuck, "Chipotle to Close All Stores on Feb. 8 for Food Safety Meeting," *NBC News*, January 15, 2016, https://www.nbcnews.com/business/business-news/chitpotle-close-all-stores-feb-8-food-safety-meeting-n497326; and Scott Neuman, "Chipotle to Retrain Employees after Latest Outbreak of Food Poisoning," *NPR*, August 17, 2018, https://www.npr.org/2018/08/17/639465193/chipotle-to-retrain-employees-after-latest-outbreak-of-food-poisoning. Bill Chappell, "Starbucks Closes More Than 8,000 Stores Today for Racial Bias Training," *NPR*, May 29, 2018, https://www.npr.org/sections/thetwo-way/2018/05/29/615119351/starbucks-closes-more-than-8-000-stores-today-for-racial-bias-training.

6. Columbia Accident Investigation Board, *Report of Columbia Accident Investigation Board, Volume I* (Washington, DC: US Government Printing Office, 2003), 200, https://www.nasa.gov/columbia/home/CAIB_Vol1.html.

7. Matthew Parsons, *Effective Knowledge Management of Law Firms* (New York: Oxford University Press, 2004), 16.

8. Ray Ryan, interview by the authors, August 23, 2020.

9. Katrina Pugh and Laurence Prusak, "Designing Effective Knowledge Networks," *Sloan Management Review* 55, no. 1 (Fall 2013): 79–88.

10. Tom Peters, *The Tom Peters Seminar: Crazy Times Call for Crazy Organizations* (New York: Vintage Books, 1994), 171.

11. Michael Trucano, "Running Your Own FAILfaire," World Bank, *EduTech blog*, November 17, 2011, https://blogs.worldbank.org/edutech/failfaire-internal.

12. Ronald Bledlow, Bernd Carette, Jana Kuehnel, and Daniela Pittig, "Learning from Others' Failures: The Effectiveness of Failure Stories for Managerial Learning," *Academy of Management Learning and Education* 16, no. 1 (2017): 40, Research Collection Lee Kong Chian School of Business, https://ink.library.smu.edu.sg/lkcsb_research_all/16.

13. Barry O'Reilly, interview by the authors, November 16, 2020.

14. This interview with Edgar Schein captures the point succinctly: Diane L. Coutu, "Edgar Schein: The Anxiety of Learning—the Darker Side of Organizational Learning," *Harvard Business School Working Knowledge*, April 15, 2002, https://hbswk.hbs.edu/archive/edgar-schein-the-anxiety-of-learning-the-darker-side-of-organizational-learning.

15. See this description of the Friction Project: https://www.bobsutton.net/friction-project/, accessed October 7, 2021.

16. Julie Makinen, "AstraZeneca: Scaling Simplification," Case HR-45, Stanford Graduate School of Business, January 15, 2018, https://stanford.edu/dept/gsb-ds/Inkling/astra.html.

17. See, for instance, Nancy Dixon, *Common Knowledge: How Companies Thrive by Sharing What They Know* (Boston: Harvard Business School Press, 2000).

18. James Somers, "The Engineers Taking on the Ventilator Shortage," *New Yorker*, May 11, 2020, https://www.newyorker.com/magazine/2020/05/18/the-engineers-taking-on-the-ventilator-shortage.

19. All VITAL quotations are from a written interview between the authors and VITAL project team members on October 30, 2020. For an overview of the VITAL project, see Taylor Hill, "How Engineers at NASA JPL Persevered to Develop a Ventilator," JPL, May 14, 2020, https://www.jpl.nasa.gov/news/news.php?feature=7661.

20. Amy C. Edmondson, Richard M. J. Bohmer, and Gary P. Pisano, "Speeding Up Team Learning," *Harvard Business Review* 79, no. 9 (October 2001): 125–134, https://hbr.org/2001/10/speeding-up-team-learning.

21. Charles Duhigg, "What Google Learned from Its Quest to Build the Perfect Team," *New York Times Magazine*, February 25, 2016, MM20.

22. Chris Argyris, "Teaching Smart People How to Learn," *Harvard Business Review* (May–June 1991): 99–109.

23. Ryan, interview.

24. James G. March, *The Ambiguities of Experience* (Ithaca, NY: Cornell University Press, 2010), 115.

25. T. K. Mattingly and Chris Scolese, private conversation with Ed Hoffman and Matt Kohut, March 2009.

26. Former US secretary of labor Robert Reich coined the term "symbolic analysts" in *Work of Nations: Preparing Ourselves for 21st-Century Capitalism* (New York: Random House, 1991).

27. For more on the NASA Academy of Program/Project & Engineering Leadership's Project HOPE, see https://appel.nasa.gov/tag/project-hope/.

28. Reid Hoffman, Ben Casnocha, and Chris Yeh, *The Alliance: Managing Talent in the Networked Age* (Boston: Harvard Business Review Press, 2014), chap. 2, Kindle.

29. Lynn Crawford, "Beyond Competence: Developing Managers of Complex Projects," in *Proceedings of AIPM National Conference* (Sydney: Australian Institute of Project Management, October 2010), 6.

30. See, for instance, NASA Academy of Program/Project & Engineering Leadership, "The Space to Collaborate, the Space to Share," *ASK the Academy* 5, no. 3 (March 6, 2012), https://appel.nasa.gov/2012/03/26/5-3_space_collaborate-html/.

Chapter 3

1. Roger Boisjoly memo to Robert K. Lund, Vice President of Engineering, Morton Thiokol, July 31, 1985, https://catalog.archives.gov/id/596263.

2. Quoted in M. Mitchell Waldrop, "NASA Responds to the Rogers Commission," *Science* 233, no. 4763 (August 1986): 512–513.

3. Presidential Commission on the Space Shuttle Challenger Accident, *Report to the President* (Washington, DC: US Government Printing Office, 1986), https://sma.nasa.gov/SignificantIncidents/assets/rogers_commission_report.pdf.

4. WJXT Films, "Challenger: A Rush to Launch," interview with Allan McDonald, 13:34–18:36, YouTube, January 28, 2016, https://www.youtube.com/watch?v=2FehGJQlOf0&t=3s.

5. "NASA Major Launch Record," NASA History Office, https://history.nasa.gov/pocketstats/sect%20B/MLR.pdf, accessed October 7, 2021.

6. For more about how the culture at NASA changed from Apollo to the space shuttle era, see Howard E. McCurdy, *Inside NASA: High Technology and Organizational Change in the US Space Program* (Baltimore, MD: Johns Hopkins Press, 1993), chapters 4–5.

7. Olivia B. Waxman, "They Were at Mission Control During Apollo 11. 50 Years Later, the Memory Still Moves Them to Tears," *TIME*, July 16, 2019, https://time.com/5623799/apollo-11-mission-control/.

8. George M. Low, introduction to *What Made Apollo a Success?*, NASA SP-287, last revised February 3, 2010, http://klabs.org/history/reports/sp287/ch1.htm.

9. "NASA Civil Service Workforce Employment Trend," NASA History Office, https://history.nasa.gov/pocketstats/sect%20D/CS%20Trend.pdf, accessed October 7, 2021.

10. Arnold S. Levine, *Managing NASA in the Apollo Era*, NASA SP-1402 (Washington, DC: US Government Printing Office, 1982), 136, https://history.nasa.gov/SP-4102.pdf.

11. "Nasa Budgets: US Spending on Space Travel Since 1958 UPDATED," *Guardian DataBlog*, https://www.theguardian.com/news/datablog/2010/feb/01/nasa-budgets-us-spending-space-travel, accessed October 7, 2021.

12. Edward W. Merrow, *Understanding the Outcomes of Megaprojects: A Quantitative Analysis of Very Large Civilian Projects* (Santa Monica, CA: RAND Corporation, 1988), 62, www.rand.org/pubs/reports/2006/R3560.pdf.

13. Samuel C. Phillips, *Summary Report of the NASA Management Study Group: Recommendations to the Administrator*, National Academy of Public Administration, December 30, 1986, 5, https://ntrs.nasa.gov/search.jsp?R=20040071104.

14. Brian Boyd, *On the Origin of Stories: Evolution, Cognition, and Fiction* (Cambridge, MA: Belknap Press of Harvard University Press, 2009), 176.

15. Jerome Bruner, "Two Modes of Thought," in *Actual Minds, Possible Worlds* (The Jerusalem-Harvard Lectures), rev. ed. (Cambridge, MA: Harvard University Press, 1987), 11–12.

16. Bruner, "Two Modes of Thought," 11–12.

17. Jamil Zaki, interview by Dan Savage, *Ten Percent Happier* podcast, episode 298, November 9, 2020, audio, 43:11.

18. Greg McKeown, *Essentialism: The Disciplined Pursuit of Less* (New York: Crown Business, 2014), 13.

19. NASA Academy of Program/Project & Engineering Leadership, "ASK OCE Interview: Five Questions for Dr. Henry Petroski," *ASK OCE* 1, no. 10 (February 26, 2010), https://appel.nasa.gov/2010/02/26/ao_1-10_f_interview-html/.

20. NASA Academy of Program/Project & Engineering Leadership, "Dennis McCarthy: The System Is Chicken," YouTube, December 1, 2010, https://www.youtube.com/watch?v=FYHwDNfyiTw.

21. Yannis Normand, "The History of the Case Study at Harvard Business School," Harvard Business School Online, *Business Insights Blog*, February 28, 2017, https://online.hbs.edu/blog/post/the-history-of-the-case-study-at-harvard-business-school.

22. Michelle Collins, "Mentors Come in All Shapes and Sizes," *ASK Magazine* 1, October 1, 2000, https://appel.nasa.gov/2000/10/01/mentors-come-in-all-shapes-and-sizes/.

23. U.S. General Accountability Office, *NASA: Better Mechanisms Needed for Sharing Lessons Learned*, GAO-02–195 (Washington, DC: US General Accountability Office, 2002), https://www.gao.gov/products/GAO-02-195.

24. Mike Ryschkewitsch, private conversation with Ed Hoffman and Matthew Kohut, May 2010.

25. NASA Academy of Program/Project & Engineering Leadership, "Collaborative Problem Solving: The STS-119 Flow Control Valve Issue," NASA, April 2013, https://appel.nasa.gov/case-studies/sts-119-html/.

26. See, for instance, Craig Warren, "'It Reads Like a Novel': The 9/11 Commission Report and the American Reading Public," *Journal of American Studies* 41, no. 3 (2007): 533–556.

27. An archive of the National Intelligence Council's "Global Trends" reports can be found here: https://www.odni.gov/index.php/ncsc-how-we-work/207-about/organization/national-intelligence-council/771-national-intelligence-council-global-trends-archive.

28. Stephen Denning, *The Springboard: How Storytelling Ignites Action in Knowledge-Era Organizations* (Boston: Butterworth-Heinemann, 2001).

29. A revised version of Simmons's book is now available: Annette Simmons, *The Story Factor: Inspiration, Influence, and Persuasion Through the Art of Storytelling* (New York: Hachette Book Group, 2019).

Chapter 4

1. Organization for Economic Cooperation and Development, *How Was Life? Global Well-Being since 1820*, ed. Jan Luiten van Zanden, Joerg Baten, Marco Mira d'Ercole, Auke Rijpma, and Marcel P. Timmer (Paris: Organization for Economic Cooperation and Development, 2014), 64, https://dx.doi.org/10.1787/9789264214262-en.

2. "2020 Best Places to Work in the Federal Government Rankings," Partnership for Public Service, https://bestplacestowork.org/rankings/overall/large, accessed October 8, 2020.

3. Ray Ryan, interview by the authors, August 23, 2020.

4. Joel Mokyr, *A Culture of Growth: The Origins of the Modern Economy* (Princeton, NJ: Princeton University Press, 2017).

5. Ryan, interview.

6. "Netflix Culture," Netflix, https://jobs.netflix.com/culture, accessed October 8, 2021; emphasis in original.

7. Robert I. Sutton, *The No Asshole Rule: Building a Civilized Workplace and Surviving One That Isn't* (New York: Business Plus, 2007).

8. Bob Sutton, "Please Help Me Update! Places and People that Use the No Asshole Rule," *Bob Sutton Work Matters* blog, February 8, 2012, https://bobsutton.typepad.com/my_weblog/2012/02/the_no_asshole_.html.

9. Don Cohen and Laurence Prusak, *In Good Company: How Social Capital Makes Organizations Work* (Boston: Harvard Business School Press, 2001).

10. Dustin Gohmert, "A New Astronaut Seat: Teamwork and Individual Initiative," *ASK Magazine* 31, June 1, 2008, https://appel.nasa.gov/2008/06/01/a-new-astronaut-seat-teamwork-and-individual-initiative/.

11. For more on social capital, see Cohen and Prusak, *In Good Company*.

12. See "Netflix Culture."

13. For more about how this worked in practice, see Justin Bariso, "Netflix's Unlimited Vacation Policy Took Years to Get Right. It's a Lesson in Emotional Intelligence," *Inc.*, September 14, 2020, https://www.inc.com/justin-bariso/netflixs-unlimited-vacation-policy-took-years-to-get-right-its-a-lesson-in-emotional-intelligence.html.

14. See, for instance, Nitin Nohria and Robert G. Eccles, "Face-to-Face: Making Network Organizations Work," in *Networks and Organizations: Structure, Form, and Action*, ed. Nitin Nohria and Robert G. Eccles (Boston, MA: Harvard Business School, 1992), 288–308.

15. Joseph Berger, "Black Jeans Invade Big Blue; First Day of a Relaxed I.B.M.," *New York Times*, February 7, 1995, B1, https://www.nytimes.com/1995/02/07/nyregion/black-jeans-invade-big-blue-first-day-of-a-relaxed-ibm.html.

16. Francis T. Hoban and Edward J. Hoffman, "An Overview of Training and Development Strategies for NASA Project Management," *PM Network* 6, no. 6 (1992): 44–49.

17. Diane Vaughan, *The Challenger Launch Decision: Risky Technology, Deviance, and Culture at NASA* (Chicago: University of Chicago Press, 1996), 62.

18. Columbia Accident Investigation Board, *Report of Columbia Accident Investigation Board, Volume I* (Washington, DC: US Government Printing Office, 2003), 130, https://www.nasa.gov/columbia/home/CAIB_Vol1.html.

Chapter 5

1. Greg R. Oldham and J. Richard Hackman, "Not What It Was and Not What It Will Be: The Future of Job Design Research," *Journal of Organizational Behavior* 3, no. 2–3 (2010): 463–479.

2. Alex "Sandy" Pentland, "The New Science of Building Great Teams," *Harvard Business Review* 90 (April 2012): 60.

3. Denise A. Bonebright, "40 Years of Storming: A Historical Review of Tuckman's Model of Small Group Development," *Human Resource Development International* 13, no. 1 (2010): 111–120.

4. See, for instance, Will Schutz, "Beyond Firo-B—Three New Theory-Derived Measures—Element B: Behavior, Element F: Feelings, Element S: Self," *Psychological Reports* 70, no. 3 (1992): 915–937, https://doi.org/10.2466/pr0.1992.70.3.915.

5. David J. Teece, Gary Pisano, and Amy Shuen, "Dynamic Capabilities and Strategic Management," *Strategic Management Journal* 18, no. 7 (August 1997): 509–533.

6. Jean-François Harvey, Henrik Bresman, Amy C. Edmondson, and Gary P. Pisano, "Team Learning and Superior Firm Performance: A Meso-Level Perspective on Dynamic Capabilities," Working Paper No. 19-059, Harvard Business School, Boston, December 2018, revised January 2020.

7. Jeff Gothelf and Josh Seiden, *Sense and Respond: How Successful Organizations Listen to Customers and Create New Products Continuously* (Boston: Harvard Business Review Press, 2017).

8. Teece, Pisano, and Shuen, "Dynamic Capabilities and Strategic Management."

9. NASA Safety Center & Office of the Chief Knowledge Officer, Goddard Space Flight Center, "STEREO: Organizational Cultures in Conflict," *Selected NASA Case Studies* (February 2009): 14–23, https://www.nasa.gov/centers/goddard/pdf/452484main_Case_Study_Magazine.pdf.

10. Charles J. Pellerin, *How NASA Builds Teams: Mission Critical Soft Skills for Scientists, Engineers, and Project Teams* (Hoboken, NJ: John Wiley & Sons, 2009), 54. This book offers an in-depth explanation of how leaders have used 4-D to conduct team interventions for NASA.

11. Terry Little, "The Goal," in *Project Management Success Stories: Lessons of Project Leaders*, ed. Alexander Laufer and Edward J. Hoffman (New York: Wiley, 2000), 120–121.

12. Karl E. Weick, *Sensemaking in Organizations* (Thousand Oaks, CA: SAGE Publications, 1995).

13. Ray Ryan, interview by the authors, August 23, 2020.

14. Connie Gersick, "Time and Transition in Work Teams: Toward a New Model of Group Development," *Academy of Management Journal* 31 (October 1988): 9–41.

15. "Nourish (*v.*)," *Merriam-Webster*, https://www.merriam-webster.com/dictionary/nourish, accessed September 30, 2021.

16. Charles Duhigg, "What Google Learned from Its Quest to Build the Perfect Team," *New York Times Magazine,* February 25, 2016, MM20.

17. Anita Woolley, Thomas W. Malone, and Christopher F. Chabris, "Why Some Teams Are Smarter than Others," *New York Times,* January 16, 2015, SR5, https://www.nytimes.com/2015/01/18/opinion/sunday/why-some-teams-are-smarter-than-others.html?.

18. Anita Woolley and Thomas W. Malone, "Defend Your Research: What Makes a Team Smarter? More Women," *Harvard Business Review* 89, no. 6 (June 2011): 32–33, http://hbr.org/2011/06/defend-your-research-what-makes-a-team-smarter-more-women/ar/1.

19. Greg Robinson, interview by the authors, November 25, 2020.

20. VITAL project team members, written interview by the authors, October 30, 2020. All VITAL quotations in this section are from this interview.

21. Scott E. Page, *The Diversity Bonus: How Great Teams Pay Off in the Knowledge Economy* (Princeton, NJ: Princeton University Press, 2017), 27.

22. Page, *The Diversity Bonus*, 32.

23. Ryan, interview.

24. Katherine W. Phillips, "What Is the Real Value of Diversity in Organizations? Questions Our Assumptions," in *The Diversity Bonus,* by Scott E. Page (Princeton, NJ: Princeton University Press, 2017), 229.

25. Jerry Madden, "What a Little Barbecue Sauce Can Do," in *Project Management Success Stories: Lessons of Project Leaders,* ed. Alexander Laufer and Edward J. Hoffman (New York: Wiley, 2000), 177–178.

26. VITAL project team members, interview.

27. Peter Temes, interview by the authors, November 9, 2020.

28. National Aeronautics and Space Administration, *International Space Station (ISS) EVA Suit Water Intrusion: High Visibility Close Call*, NASA, IRIS Case Number: S-2013-199-00005, December 20, 2013, https://www.nasa.gov/sites/default/files/files/Suit_Water_Intrusion_Mishap_Investigation_Report.pdf.

29. NASA Academy of Program/Project & Engineering Leadership, "Redesigning the Cosmic Background Explorer," NASA, January 2009, https://www.nasa.gov/pdf/384131main_COBE_case_study.pdf.

30. Kathryn B. McEwen and Carolyn M. Boyd, "A Measure of Team Resilience: Developing the Resilience at Work Team Scale," *Journal of Occupational and Environmental Medicine* 60, no. 3 (2018): 258–272, https://doi.org/10.1097/JOM.0000000000001223.

31. Carol S. Dweck, *Mindset: The New Psychology of Success* (New York: Ballantine Books, 2006).

32. Sherin Shibu and Shana Lebowitz, "Microsoft Is Rolling Out a New Management Framework to Its Leaders. It Centers around a Psychological Insight Called Growth Mindset," *Business Insider*, November 11, 2019, https://www.businessinsider .com/microsoft-is-using-growth-mindset-to-power-management-strategy-2019-11. See also Robert Martin, "Resilience Message: Change Your Mindset, Change Your World," US Army War College Archives, August 23, 2016, https://www.armywarcollege.edu /news/Archives/12534.pdf.

33. Iain Hamilton, interview by the authors, November 6, 2020.

34. Martin E. P. Seligman, *Flourish: A Visionary New Understanding of Happiness and Well-Being* (New York: Free Press, 2011).

Chapter 6

1. "International Space Station Facts and Figures," NASA, last updated September 7, 2021, https://www.nasa.gov/feature/facts-and-figures.

2. *ASK Magazine* staff, "The Challenge of Collaboration," *ASK Magazine* 47, August 1, 2012, https://appel.nasa.gov/2012/08/01/the-challenge-of-collaboration/.

3. Don Cohen, "Interview with William Gerstenmaier," *ASK Magazine* 38, April 12, 2010, https://appel.nasa.gov/2010/04/12/interview-with-william-gerstenmaier/.

4. "Shuttle-Mir Background: Negotiations and Joint Planning," *History of Shuttle-Mir*, NASA Johnson Space Center, last updated September 9, 2021, https://historycollection .jsc.nasa.gov/history/shuttle-mir/history/h-before.htm.

5. David Baker, *International Space Station: 1998–2011 (All Stages)* (Somerset, UK: Haynes Publishing Group, 2012).

6. John McBrine, interview by Don Cohen, October 30, 2020.

7. Kerry Ellis, "International Life Support," *ASK Magazine* 44, November 2, 2011, https://appel.nasa.gov/2011/11/02/international-life-support/.

8. Cady Coleman, interview by Don Cohen, September 22, 2020.

9. Don Cohen, "Interview with Lynn Cline," *ASK Magazine* 48, November 1, 2012, https://appel.nasa.gov/2012/11/01/interview-with-lynn-cline/. All quotations are from this interview until noted otherwise.

10. "NASA Headquarters Oral History Project Edited Oral History Transcript: Lynn F. H. Cline," interviewed by Sandra Johnson, NASA JSC, March 17, 2016, https:// historycollection.jsc.nasa.gov/JSCHistoryPortal/history/oral_histories/NASA_HQ /Administrators/ClineLFH/ClineLFH_3-17-16.htm.

11. "NASA Headquarters Oral History Project."

12. "Masters with Masters 9: Bill Gerstenmaier and Kuniaki Shiraki," hosted by the NASA Academy of Program/Project & Engineering Leadership, Washington, DC, July 11, 2011, YouTube, uploaded July 12, 2011, https://www.youtube.com/watch?v=KXB2qg9XpCc.

13. Cohen, "Interview with Lynn Cline."

14. "NASA Headquarters Oral History."

15. Cohen, "Interview with Lynn Cline."

16. Tim Howell, "In Their Own Words: Preserving International Space Station Knowledge," *ASK Magazine* 36, September 1, 2009, https://appel.nasa.gov/2009/09/01/in-their-own-words-preserving-international-space-station-knowledge/.

17. Cohen, "Interview with William Gerstenmaier."

18. Coleman, interview.

19. Cohen, "Interview with William Gerstenmaier."

20. For more about the international project management course, see: https://appel.nasa.gov/course-catalog/appel-ipm/.

Chapter 7

1. John Kay and Mervyn King, *Radical Uncertainty: Decision-Making Beyond the Numbers* (New York: W. W. Norton, 2020), 14.

2. Philip Tetlock's groundbreaking book *Expert Political Judgment: How Good Is It? How Can We Know?* (Princeton, NJ: Princeton University Press, 2005) and subsequent studies have demonstrated the paucity of accuracy in political predictions by "experts." His findings could also be applied to economics (how many analysts failed to anticipate the Great Recession?) and management.

3. See National Aeronautics and Space Administration, *NOAA N-Prime Mishap Investigation: Final Report*, NASA, September 13, 2004, https://www.nasa.gov/pdf/65776main_noaa_np_mishap.pdf; and Jason Bates, "Lockheed Martin Profits to Pay for NOAA N-Prime Repairs," *Space*, October 11, 2004, https://www.space.com/417-lockheed-martin-profits-pay-noaa-prime-repairs.html.

4. We are grateful to our colleague Yahiro Takegami of IBM Japan for this insight.

5. Barry O'Reilly, *Unlearn: Let Go of Past Success to Achieve Extraordinary Results* (New York: McGraw-Hill, 2019).

6. David Epstein, *Range: How Generalists Triumph in a Specialized World* (New York: Riverhead Books, 2019), 34.

7. Chen Zhang, David M Mayer, and Eunbit Hwang, "More Is Less: Learning but Not Relaxing Buffers Deviance under Job Stressors," *Journal of Applied Psychology* 103, no. 2 (February 2018):123–136, https://doi.org/10.1037/apl0000264.

8. This formulation draws from the definition used by Brian Cantwell Smith in *The Promise of Artificial Intelligence: Reckoning and Judgment* (Cambridge, MA: MIT Press, 2019), xv.

9. Lilah Burke, "Google Releases New IT Certificate," *Inside Higher Ed*, January 17, 2020, https://www.insidehighered.com/quicktakes/2020/01/17/google-releases-new -it-certificate.

10. Noel Tichy, former head of GE's leadership academy, offered this definition of leadership in Noel M. Tichy with Eli Cohen, *The Leadership Engine: How Winning Companies Build Leaders at Every Level* (New York: HarperCollins, 1997).

Index